Cliff Parker has written humorously on the subject of fishing for many years. Formerly a regular contributor to 'Angling Times' and 'Angler's Mail', he has also written a number of bestselling fishing books, including 'The Fishing Handbook to End All Fishing Handbooks', 'Hook, Line and Stinker' and 'The Compleat Wally Angler', available in Sphere Books.

The Angler's Bedside, Bankside and Barside Yearbook

Cliff Parker

SPHERE BOOKS LIMITED

Also by Cliff Parker in Sphere Books:

FISHING FOR LAFFS
THE FISHING HANDBOOK TO END
   ALL FISHING HANDBOOKS
HOOK, LINE AND STINKER
SLING YOUR HOOK
THE COMPLEAT WALLY ANGLER

Illustration Acknowledgements

Line drawings of fish are by Graham Allen, reproduced from
Teach Yourself Coarse Angling by Cliff Parker, courtesy of
Hodder & Stoughton Educational, with the exception of the
salmon (p. 17), trout (p. 26) and bleak (p. 16) which have been
drawn for this book.
The photograph on p. 46 is reproduced by kind
permission of *Angling Times*.
The photograph on p. 99 is reproduced by kind permission of
Ritchie McDonald.

Sphere Books Limited, 27 Wrights Lane, London w8 5tz
First published in Great Britain by Sphere Books Ltd 1987
© Cliff Parker 1987

Set in 10/12 pt Sabon by
Rowland Phototypesetting Limited
Bury St Edmunds, Suffolk

Printed and bound in Great Britain by
Billing and Sons Ltd Worcester

The Angler's Bedside, Bankside and Barside Yearbook

The Angler's Guide to January

January is a depressing month in any sphere of activity. Christmas and New Year celebrations are over, leaving behind mass outbreaks of ill-disposition and severe hangovers. Every post brings a new crop of horrific bills. The weather is usually wet, windy and bitterly cold. There's nothing to laff at at all.

The turnout for the annual New Year fishing match is, if anything, even less than that for Boxing Day (see December). And the results are even more abysmal, with almost a whole fortnight of merrymaking exacting its toll of cack-handed casting, unnoticed bites, missed strikes and falling in the water.

But take heart. In the words of Bernard Venables, introducing the immortal angler Mr Crabtree, there are joys in winter fishing which belie the general impression of nature being held in a deep, cold sleep.

'In winter,' he wrote, 'the otter may still be seen by the lucky fisherman. The heron still stalks about the shallows . . . The kingfisher and the dipper have not departed, and in fact the dipper sings more sweetly from December on than it does at any other time . . .'

The hardy January fisherman, then, can sit swaddled on his basket and, as he waits for bites, listen to the sweet song of the energetic dipper. As the bird's cheerful call penetrates the fug of his hangover, he greets it with the time-honoured salutation to one of nature's liveliest and chirpiest creations: 'You noisy little swine! Bugger off . . .'

One of the consolations of winter fishing is that certain fish have hardened up, grown bigger and stronger, and are at the peak of fighting condition.

The roach, for instance, hardly renowned as a scrapper, will emerge as a well-muscled fighter. So will the rudd, more usually thought of as a summer fish.

A winter chub is a different fish altogether from the finicky and often spiritless thing of the summer. This is the time when even medium-sized chub smash the unwary angler time after time with a sudden dive for a tangle of roots, leaving the angler lost in admiration for their fighting qualities and in a rosy afterglow of the memories of their titanic struggles. (That's the official version, anyway. How it really leaves him is muttering, cursing, in a foul temper and just in the mood to get wellied when he reaches the pub.)

The pike, above all, is at the peak of its powers. There is no way that a winter pike gives in without fighting to the last inch of line.

Even when grassed, it makes one last desperate gesture of defiance. In the bitter January weather, the angler's fingers are stiff and clumsy, making disgorging a tricky and sometimes hit-and-miss operation. When the pike takes a snap at his fumbling fingers, it makes sure it *doesn't* miss.

The angler has one consolation. With his hands as numb as they are, he doesn't feel the pain so much. Not until he's thawing out in the pub afterwards and asking for 'A pint of – Aaarrrggghhh!!!!'

Some New Year Resolutions for Well-Meaning Anglers

I solemnly resolve that in the New Year and indeed for ever more:

1. I shall not keep maggots in the fridge unless they be securely packed and prominently labelled.
2. I shall not raid the larder for bait without prior consultation and receipt of the necessary permission.
3. I shall not squidge worms in the blender as a groundbait additive. Not without washing the blender out afterwards, anyway.
4. I shall not fish too close to fellow anglers, nor pinch their pre-baited swims, nor prevail upon them to lend me such necessaries as maggots, floats, hooks and shot.
5. I shall not use aids to my match techniques which may not be strictly in accordance with the rules, such as throwing soap surreptitiously into my opponent's swim, distracting his attention as his float bobs, or using artificial enhancements to my catch weight such as the odd spiral lead.
6. In recounting tales of my fishing prowess to my fellow anglers, I shall not stretch the truth more than is necessary to produce an interesting account and suitable dramatic effect.
7. I shall not nick the tackle of my long-suffering sons without first asking permission, nor shall I return it in anything other than mint condition.
8. I shall be more considerate of my wife and family; shall not depart noisily and return even more noisily, smelling of the Demon Drink, falling over the milk bottles and wiping my feet on the cat.
9. On my return I shall not just dump everything in a heap for the little woman to clear away, but shall wash out all nets, dispose of surplus bait, and put my tackle and gear away in a tidy and responsible manner.
10. I shall not bring my stalwart comrades home from the pub after a hard-fought match to disturb the peace of the neighbourhood and the sleep of my wife and family. Should I do so in a moment of forgetfulness, I will not allow them to doss down in the living room to the detriment of the peace of mind of the family and the cat first thing next morning.

Follow those few simple rules, lads, and you'll have a trouble-free year. The one snag is that resolutions such as these do not have all that long a life; by the end of the first weekend in January there are usually very few of them left. But at least you tried.

I Say, I Say, I Say . . .

The match team came down from the North and won an important trophy against a London team. After the match, they had a wild night of celebration in the capital.

Harold met a young lady in Soho and they spent the night together in a hotel separate from the rest of the team. Next morning, his wife rang his original hotel room and could get no reply. So she sent a telegram to every member of the team asking if they knew where he was.

She had thirty telegrams in reply, all saying: 'DON'T WORRY. HAROLD SPENT NIGHT WITH ME.'

Our match team can lose ten contests in a row. But is it down-hearted? No! It pitches right back in and loses another ten.

Fishing Through the Ages

This ancient Japanese print is said to depict an ancient Japanese method of reviving ancient Japanese anglers who have fallen in the water. Other experts have claimed that it depicts:

   (a) An angler whose eyesight was not up to the difference between a bullock and a bull.

   (b) An angler set on his way by his mates after overdoing the Demon Drink on a club social night.

   (c) An angler attempting to beat the drink-and-drive laws.

   (d) An angler working up to another story that nobody's going to believe.

It's a Fact

Dry-Net Giveaway

In January 1987 a Yorkshire angler left his wife to set up home with his lover after his wife caught him out. He visited the other woman under the pretext of going fishing – but his wife became suspicious because his tackle never got wet.

Confucius he say,
Man who sit on rod rest
Quickly go up in world.

Know Your Fish

Chub (*Leuciscus cephalus*)

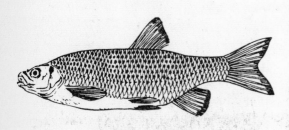

According to the book:
Bulky, cautious, hard-fighting fish. Likes moving water. Lurks in holes or hollows, among roots or under trees. Feeds at any hour of day or night and, once its suspicions are allayed, takes almost anything: slugs, worms, crayfish, bread, grasshoppers and cheese.
Record: 7 lb 6 oz (3.345 kg)
Between ourselves:
The chub takes as much loose feed as you care to throw in, but spits out anything it thinks has a hook in it. If it does get hooked it dives for the most snagful cover it can find. Tackle dealers owe a great deal of their prosperity to the loonies who go dapping for summer chub on treed-up banks.

Dace (*Leuciscus leuciscus*)

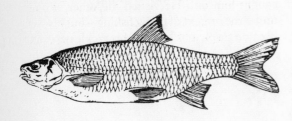

According to the book:
Slim, frisky, silvery shoal fish, fond of fast-running water. Good fighting fish for its size.

Surface and midwater feeder in warm weather, bottom feeder in colder weather. Feeds on through the winter. Likes maggots, worms, hemp, bread and elderberries. Will also take small, flashy spoons.
Record: 1 lb 4 oz 4 dms (0.574 kg)
Between ourselves:
A bit of a pest if you're after something bigger, but otherwise there's not a lot nasty you can say about it. Seems a happy little thing. Often a face-saver when the temperature drops, but doesn't look over-impressive on photographs or in the keep net.

It's a Fact

Everybody's Doing It

Fishing is Britain's biggest participant sport, with 4,000,000 devotees. More people go fishing every weekend than watch professional football. And 15 per cent of all households in Britain contain at least one angler.

It's not the completely male preserve many people think it is: one in fifteen anglers is a woman. Nor is it entirely the gentle, harmless recreation of popular image: in 1982 it killed more people than any other single sport or leisure activity, mainly through drowning accidents.

Knock, knock.
Who's there?
Adrian.
Adrian who?
Adrian my trousers 'cos I fell in the water.

Knock, knock.
Who's there?
Lloyd.
Lloyd who?
He Lloyd to everyone in the pub about the size of his fish.

Know Your Tackle

The Rod

There are two basic kinds of rod:

1. The dull-coloured, matt-finished one with dark whippings. This rod, practically invisible from under water, catches fish, which many anglers believe to be the prime purpose of the operation.
2. The rod that novices prefer – the light-coloured, highly varnished one with fluorescent whippings. This rod catches anglers. It looks very impressive when you're waving it about, but sends out signals which every fish recognises, i.e.: Flash Harry's on the bank.

When buying a rod, it's best to try a few practice casts in the shop to test its feel and balance. Tackle dealers are used to this and are not at all surprised when a vigorous back swing clears all the stock off the top shelf, and an expertly flicked sideways cast pokes the next customer's eye out. Rumour has it that dealers make more profit from charging the angler for the broken shop-soiled stock on the top shelf than from selling the rod itself. And they're insured against lawsuits from one-eyed customers.

Most rods have three sections, or joints. Otherwise you'd never get the things on the bus. The sections are joined by metal bits called ferrules. Ferrules are designed so that they connect up easily enough, but stick irretrievably when you try to unship the rod.

A *through-action* rod is one which bends into the middle joint. A *tip-action* rod is one in which only the top joint bends. The through-action absorbs the lunges of the fish better and looks more spectacular, making it ideal for beginners and show-offs. The tip-action gives a faster strike and a better 'feel' to the fish, resulting in the traditional angler's cry of 'Ohmygawd! It's a whopper!' at the first tug of an undernourished gudgeon.

Take several rods of different types with you, especially in changeable weather, so that you can cope with most conditions on the water. Sod's Law decrees that the rod you need for any given condition is the one you've left at home or lent to your mate.

It's a Fact

Soap Hoax, Foax

Brookside's anglers are dead fishy

A VILLAGE fell hook, line and sinker for the Brookside anglers.

Two men claiming to be from the Channel 4 soap opera arrived in a white van and began setting up fishing tackle at the side of a busy road.

After fixing dead fish to their hooks, a third man filmed as they landed them from a grid in the gutter.

Conned

Having told the watching crowd, in Rainhill, Merseyside, not to miss the scene on TV, they sped off.

But last night a Brookside spokesman said: "They have been conned. We weren't out on location."

The Daily Star, 27 January 1984.

It's a Fact

More Water with It

In Oklahoma, USA, it is illegal to get a fish drunk.

The Things They Said . . .

The Good, the Bad and the Stupid

There is something in fishing that is relative to holiness. It makes men good-tempered and quiet-minded. It steadies the nerves and sweetens the understanding . . . A bad man was never a good fisher, and probably never a fisher at all, undesirous even of wetting a line.

Herbert Palmer,
The Roving Angler (1933)

But before you get too smug about it:

. . . the cruelest, the coldest, and the stupidest of pretended sports . . . The whale, the shark, and the tunny fishery have somewhat of noble and perilous in them; even net fishing, trawling etc., are more human and useful. But angling! No angler can be a good man.

Lord Byron (1788–1824)

With a nickname like 'The Bad Lord Byron', he certainly had no room to talk about other people. He was a devil with the women, among other things, being a shade more handsome than the average angler. Came to a sticky end in Greece, which some reckon served him right, though it could have been the cooking that did it. If he'd stayed at home and gone fishing, he'd probably have lasted longer.

Who Runs the Club?

The angling club is a great British institution, even though the first recorded one was the Schuylkill Fishing Company, Philadelphia, Pa, USA, formed as long ago as 1732.

British fishing clubs as we know them, devoted mainly to coarse fishing, came into existence early in the nineteenth century after the Industrial Revolution.

The notion held by many anglers' wives that they were formed for the sole purpose of lying and boozing is, in fact, correct. The early clubs were less concerned with fishing rights than with just getting together for an hour or so of convivial chat and boasting over a few jars.

Today, however, the club is a far more complex organisation. Though members often take its existence for granted, it does not run itself: its smooth operation depends on a dedicated bunch of officials, willing to give their time and expertise for the benefit of their fellow men and in the hope of the occasional free pint.

Each month throughout this book gives the functions of some of these stalwart officials, as a guide to anyone thinking of standing for election. Though the magnitude of the tasks may deter some, others may see them as a challenge, and become all the more determined to stand. And at least they can't say that nobody warned them.

The Secretary

If you can keep your head when all about you
Are losing theirs and blaming it on you

. . . you're probably the club secretary.

Your job basically is as archivist and recorder of the club's activities. Sounds easy enough. What it means in fact is that you're involved in everything, from the safekeeping and interpretation of the club's legal documents to ensuring that the bingo tickets and pork pies arrive in time for social nights.

Should anything go wrong, no matter which official or committee holds responsibility, the fault is always traced back to you.

If you can keep your head when all about you
Are losing theirs and blaming it on you,
You just don't understand the situation.

. . . So says a panicking social committee chairman when the pies don't turn up and the beer runs out. You should have reminded him. You did remind him? Well, you should have reminded him again. Is he supposed to think of everything? Has he got a crystal ball? Is it his fault if you allow the membership to consist entirely of raving dipsos who would sup the Grand Union Canal dry if it were filled with draught bitter? Whose idea of a varied diet is four revolting pies and three packets of smoky-bacon crisps? Who are now banging on the tables, singing 'Why Are We Waiting?' and threatening to wreck the place if something doesn't turn up? That's his fault? That's *your* fault.

It's the secretary's fault when the minutes of the last meeting are read out and from the floor come cries of 'Rubbish!', 'Nowt like it!' and 'I never said that!'

Your fault when the bills arrive from scattered hostelries, asking reimbursement for accounts members put on the slate in the name of the club. Your fault again when members' signatures on the bills are deciphered as D. Duck, N. Bonaparte, M. Mouse and Sid Gorbachev. That's a problem for the treasurer? Oh no, it's not. False pretences. Dodgy. Outside his jurisdiction, old lad. Down to you, that is.

Your fault yet again when the clubhouse telephone and heating bills hit astronomical heights. Nothing to do with the fact that Shifty Sid Shorthouse has been using the phone to place bets on forthcoming fishing matches and call his brother in Australia. Nor that after illicit boozing sessions, the members were too far gone to remember to turn the heating off, leaving it going full blast in an empty club for the next week.

That electricity bill. Bit steep, old son. Perhaps you'd better attend to the correspondence at home in future. And talking about that: the money that's been spent on stationery. £3.50 for notepaper and envelopes? Are you trying to bankrupt the club? And what's all this spent on stamps? You're not actually putting *stamps* on the envelopes? The bloke before you never did. Used to stick the letters in his firm's post tray, that's what *he* did.

It is a fact that many a club secretary stays in the job for years. This is ascribed to enthusiasm, devotion to duty, a wish to serve the club to the best of his ability for as long as he can. Or that nobody else is masochist enough to stand for election.

It is a fact, too, that often a secretary represents the public image of the club to the members, to related associations and federations, and to the outside world.

Harassed, haunted, careworn, baggy-eyed, down-at-heel, hair falling out, divorce pending . . . Yes, the image is all-important.

Still:

If you can keep your head when all about you . . .

Knock knock.
Who's there?
Athol.
Athol who?
Athol'd my rodth, tho I can't come fithing.

Knock, knock.
Who's there?
Canoe.
Canoe who?
Canoe come fishing, or won't oo' wife let you?

The Things They Said . . .

Putting Some Bite In It

Dr Strabismus (Whom God Preserve) of Utrecht is carrying out research work with a view to crossing salmon with mosquitoes. He says it will mean a bite every time for fishermen.

J. B. Morton
Beachcomber: a January tailpiece

Hints for Club Officials

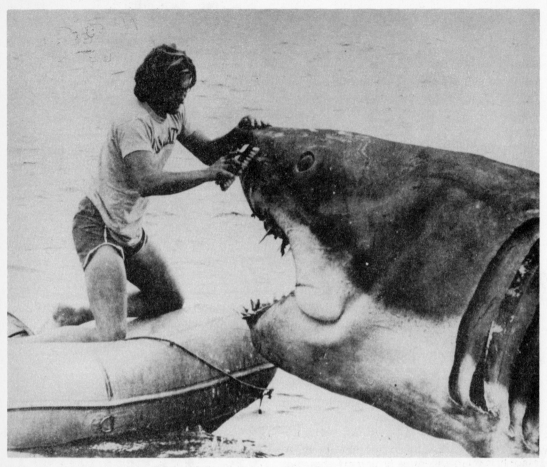

Get your team's catch looking its best. I mean, look at the state of that shark. Glassy-eyed, bits of person all over its nose, teeth in a filthy mess. It'll never get into *Jaws* if it carries on looking like this.

Your Luck in the Stars

Of *course* you don't believe in horoscopes. Load of old rubbish. How can the fact that Mars is in conjunction with Uranus mean that on January 15 you'll catch a 5 lb chub and meet a tall dark bailiff? Having unfortunately forgotten to buy a ticket?

Codswallop. But it is accepted that people born at different times of the year tend to have different characteristics. And this is what we're looking at: your birth sign and how it affects your temperament and abilities as an angler.

A detailed prognostication is given in each monthly section. But just to get you interested, or to save you reading further, here's a brief rundown:

AQUARIUS (*January 21–February 19*)
A lovely feller. Top-flight angler and original tackle designer. But far too generous. The target of every cadger in the club.
PISCES (*February 20–March 20*)
Hopeless. Daydreams while his float bobs. Often caught fiddling a match result. Spends more time in the boozer than on the bank.
ARIES (*March 21–April 20*)
Loves the Great Outdoors. Fishes on the move and usually gets results. Accident-prone. Returns home in less than mint condition.
TAURUS (*April 21–May 21*)
Fishes steadily. Does well. Takes no rubbish from stewards or bailiffs. Runs to fat and falls through bottoms of boats.
GEMINI (*May 22–June 21*)
Seldom sits still, seldom shuts up. Not above faking a result. Doesn't catch a lot, but to hear him talk you'd never know.
CANCER (*June 22–July 23*)
Frets a lot. Has a lot to fret about. Shy, retiring, cack-handed. Falls in the water. But at the full of the moon, watch out for him . . .
LEO (*July 24–August 23*)
Born show-off. Fibs like mad about his catch. Likes his ale and tends to overdo it. Is often taken home in a wheelbarrow.

VIRGO (*August 24–September 23*)
Fussy, pernickety, pedantic. Isn't over-keen on fishing, but likes the detail involved in club organisation. A pain in the bum.
LIBRA (*September 24–October 23*)
A proper Dapper Dan. Never gets wet or muddy unless other members throw him in the water. They do this quite a lot.
SCORPIO (*October 24–November 22*)
Rough, tough, always right. Does everything to excess. Never pinch his pre-baited swim if you value your front teeth.
SAGITTARIUS (*November 23–December 21*)
Slapdash angler. Catches fish in spite of himself. Falls in the water more often than he should. Gets home happy, but unfit for human consumption.
CAPRICORN (*December 22–January 20*)
Methodical, single-minded. Takes everything too seriously. Not over-popular on account of miserly ways and miserable expression.

Aquarius (*January 21–February 19*)

Too true to be bad

If you didn't exist, Aquarius, you'd have to be invented. You put the rest of us to shame.

You're the nicest, brightest sign in the zodiac, and the average fishing club doesn't deserve you. You are taken advantage of something rotten.

For starters, you are the zodiac's one completely unselfish character. A fool to yourself.

God's gift to the cadger. If anyone wanders up to your pitch, asking in wheedling tones whether you could lend him a handful of maggots, a couple of worms, a bag of groundbait, he gets them. By the time you've asked what his other needs are, he's loaded up with everything on his first shopping list. Plus half a dozen hooks, three floats, an assortment of non-toxic weights in various sizes, the loan of your landing net and a couple of cheese-and-pickle butties on account of he forgot to bring his own. If it's raining, he's gone away clad in your spare anorak. Which you will never see again, but what the hell?

You can be either an A-Team matchman or a top-flight specimen hunter. Sometimes you turn out to be both, which nobody believes. Not that the disbelief bothers you; you're a dealer in truth, and if you've done it you've done it. Otherwise you wouldn't have admitted it. And admitting it is all you do; you certainly don't boast about it.

Yours is the sign of the archetypal absent-minded professor. Far-seeing and inventive, you produce idea after idea for new baits, new techniques and new tackle. All of which you forget to patent or protect. In twelve months' time you're intrigued to see that a cowboy-tackle firm is producing one of your inventions in highly profitable quantities without a brass farthing going to you. You're a bit sad, perhaps, but not too upset; you've got a dozen more ideas where that came from. You forget to patent those as well.

Never a snappy dresser, you wear what's comfortable. You turn up to collect your prize as Fisherman of the Year wearing a bobbly hat, string vest (no shirt) and odd socks. So? You won the prize for your angling skills, not for your sartorial elegance. Leave that to Libra. Just a pity you forgot your trousers.

Your tackle is always in good order. You keep it clean and functional, not in the old-maid fashion of Virgo nor the dog-in-the-manger style of Capricorn, but like a no-nonsense craftsman who recognises the need to take good care of his tools.

If anything's broken, it doesn't stay broken for long. You can take the most highly complicated reel to pieces, clean and oil all the parts, replace any worn or broken bits and – here's the real test – put everything back together again.

You treat your catches kindly. The pain to a fish – properly hooked, played, handled and returned to the water – is, as your scientific mind has squared with your well-developed conscience, minimal. So you make sure that the whole operation is carried out with care and respect.

You treat people kindly. The biggest bores, the most pompous officials, the most frantic trophy-hunters, the most neurotic matchmen; they're all treated with the same tolerance, sympathy and good humour that you give your best friends.

Friends? Because your standards are high, your principles firm, you don't make friends instantly or by the dozen. But you make them steadily over the years. And Aquarius for a friend is a friend for life. Always there, always dependable, always generous, always a help in time of trouble.

Perhaps the only thing a friend can't depend on is your day-to-day practicality. You're a bit vague, as befits the absent-minded professor. So it was probably an Aquarian who inspired the creaky old joke of the bloke who was sent by his mate to get the provisions for the fishing trip. He returned with two loaves of bread and six bottles of Scotch.

'Hell!' said his mate. 'Can't I leave anything to you?'

'What's the matter?' said Aquarius.

'What's the matter? Six bottles of Scotch and two loaves! What the hell are we going to do with all that bread?'

OK . . . it's a creaky old joke. But you can't leave Aquarius looking as if he's perfect. It would embarrass him . . .

What Do You Know?

This is:
(a) A very thin fish.
(b) A fish not in the peak of condition.
(c) A potential record-breaker left lying about where the cat could get at it.
(d) The result of putting a perch in a netful of pike.

(e) A fish which caused some suspicion at the weigh-in.
(f) The last inhabitant of Idiots' Reach.
(g) A fish without any clothes on.

Whichever conclusion you come to, go and have a pint. After wasting time answering silly bloody questions like these, you deserve it.

Great Angling Loonies

Willow Wally

Eighteenth-century scholar Thomas Birch (1705–66) was a keen angler but a lousy one. In an effort to do better, he built himself a tree outfit, with branches into which he shoved his arms, and knotholes through which he could see.

Dressed like this, he waddled down to the river bank and fished away, a sitting – or standing – target for every passing dog. He still didn't catch anything, which was a pity, because he was the father of angling camouflage as we know it.

As his biography describes Birch's experi-

ments: 'In this sylvan attire he used to take root by the side of a favourite stream, and imagined that his motions might seem to the fish to be the effect of the wind. He pursued this amusement for some years in the same habit, till he was ridiculed out of it by his friends.'

With friends like that . . .

Perhaps poor old Birch would have been better sticking to his harmless pursuit. He died in London on 9 January 1766 after falling off his horse. Seems he wasn't much good at horse-riding, either.

Don't Forget to Write

The art of letter writing, though threatened in the computer age, is thankfully not yet dead. A correctly addressed, well-phrased letter is a powerful instrument of communication. It can make complicated arrangements, put forward detailed explanations, clinch business deals, offer friendship, hospitality and condolences.

Angling club officials, especially the secretary, should aim for proficiency in letter writing as an aid to a quieter life and the more efficient running of the club. The individual angler, too, will find that his path can be smoothed by a well-turned phrase.

Here, and at intervals throughout the book, are presented sample letters dealing with delicate situations which the club and the individual angler are likely to encounter in the course of a year.

It's no use saying, 'It couldn't happen to me.' It may already have. Just wait for the next post . . .

Making the Peace

Club secretaries are often called upon to make the peace with publicans after social events have got a little out of hand. This kind of thing tends to happen mostly over the Yuletide festive season, when spirits are high and members behave with uncharacteristic boisterousness.

The tone of the letter should be conciliatory, but should admit no more liability than is absolutely necessary. Blame for the incident should be deflected as far as possible on to persons other than club members.

> Edward Fanshawe, Esq.,
> Licensee,
> The Bricklayer's Arms,
> Foundry Road,
> Sludgethorpe.

Dear Mr Fanshawe,
As Secretary of the Sludgethorpe Waltonians, I am writing in an endeavour to clear up the little misunderstanding last month which has resulted in your good self banning members of our association from your hostelry.

On behalf of the social committee, I readily admit that one of our members was guilty of spilling several pint glasses of draught bitter on the carpet in an attempt to drink them standing on his head. He has since been suspended from the club and will not be reinstated until he has made appropriate restitution.

I admit also that another of our members was responsible for tipping a canful of maggots down the corsage of your good lady wife, giving the aforesaid corsage a slap which squashed quite a number of the creatures, and singing a song which may unwittingly have caused offence. (The phrase 'a lovely bunch of coconuts' was in no way intended as a reference to your lady wife's physique.) This member, too, has been suspended until he has made his personal apologies and paid for the cleaning bills involved, plus an *ex gratia* payment which may go some way towards assuaging your lady wife's hurt feelings.

But as to who left the dead pike hanging behind the door of the ladies' toilet (to the discomfiture, I understand, of your barmaid, Miss Maisie Fruit), I can only hazard a guess. Without casting any aspersions, I suspect that it was the work of members of Slagville Piscatorials, several of whom were in your hostelry on the night in question, and who are noted for their anti-social and often rowdy behaviour.

Certainly it was they who made the disparaging remarks about our members' angling prowess, which caused the tables in the public bar to be overturned and the ashtrays to be thrown.

The setting fire to the curtains was certainly unfortunate, and though the lighted match was in the grasp of one of our members, he could hardly be blamed for falling backwards off his seat after being struck by a flying ashtray.

Time is a great healer, and I hope that enough has elapsed since that unfortunate night for you to reconsider your decision and once again allow our members access to the facilities of your excellent hostelry.

Assuring you of our members' best behaviour at all future times, I remain,
Yours sincerely,
Eli Witherspoon,
Secretary, Sludgethorpe Waltonians
Angling Club.

As Others See Us

Is there such a thing as an average angler? Difficult question. But a survey has shown that the *composite* angler is more likely to be under thirty-five than over, has a higher-than-average income, owns or has the use of a car, and spends hundreds of pounds a year on tackle, bait, permits and travel.

He goes fishing, it says here, for adventure, excitement and mental relaxation. A minority of anglers, possibly the honest ones, replied that they went fishing to get away from the wife. The composite angler will sometimes take his son with him but not, if he can help it, his wife or daughter.

Fishing is the main purpose of the trip: eating and drinking are normally the only other activities indulged in. (Perhaps night fishing was not included in the survey.) So the wives left at home at least have the consolation that hubby isn't getting up to much.

The wives, instead, may have been quite pleased to have the husbands out from under their feet, and happy about 'the sport's beneficial effect on the husbands' general demeanour'. The only drawback about that opinion is that all who agreed with it were men.

The social scientists conducting the survey summed it up thus: 'The current norm of the angling sub-culture appears to run contrary to current social trends.'

Which, elaborated on, meant that they thought the composite angler to be selfish, self-centred, anti-social and indifferent to concepts of sex equality, togetherness and family-shared recreation.

What a thing to say . . .

Angling's Big Questions

Why Do Anglers Fib?

Anglers are prone to telling lies. A sad reflection on the practitioners of the Noble Art, but unfortunately true. Psychologists have come up with several reasons for it, including:

POETIC LICENCE
Every angler is a poet at heart, and so given to the poet's natural habit of embellishing the boring old truth to make a story worth listening to. Who wants to hear about a one-eyed gudgeon, for God's sake?

COMPETITIVE SPIRIT
It's a cruel, hard world we live in, with every man trying to prove that he's the greatest. So when those around you are boasting nineteen to the dozen, what are *you* supposed to do?

CREDIBILITY GAP
Nobody believes an angler, anyway, least of all his fellow anglers. So it's no use telling them you landed a 20 lb carp: they'll knock a good third off the weight for starters. Tell 'em you caught a 30 lb carp. By the time they've finished their mental arithmetic, they'll have got it right.

INFLUENCE OF THE MEDIA
Open any angling publication and what do you see? Monstrous fish being smirked over by immodest captors. These, you are told, are the only fish worth taking notice of. Makes you spit.

FAULTY OBSERVATION
A fish always looks bigger underwater, especially if it's fighting hard. Often all the angler sees of a fish which breaks him is a flash of scales from its flanks. Who's to *say* it's not four feet long?

SENSORY DEPRIVATION
Sitting all day cocooned in weatherproof clothing causes sensory deprivation, one common symptom of which is hallucination. Nothing like a good hallucination to tell in the pub. Which brings us to:

THE DEMON DRINK
Now that's a bit more like . . .

The Angler's Guide to February

February is not called February Filldyke for nothing. It's called that because for most of the month it's bucketing down. The rain and melting snow fill the canals and rivers to overflowing.

It's a month when the fish seek out the deep holes and bankside eddies to stay out of the current. They're often a bit grumpy and off their food because of the suspended silt which irritates their gills, but they can be tempted with the tail of a lob fished ledger on the bottom.

Now and again a river will overflow its banks, and the fish will follow the water up into the fields, feeding on the worms and grubs in the grass. They are pursued there by the hardier and dafter anglers with some degree of success. And a fish that was actually caught in a field makes a better story than one that was caught in the boring old river.

The trick is to study the river when it's not in flood and make notes of the topography of the bank, so that you'll know how far down the field you can walk in safety. When you have waded to the bottom of the field, however, you may find yourself a little disorientated or suffering from temporary amnesia. You may also find that a spur of bank you remember perfectly well is not there any more.

Insurance companies, as a matter of general policy, are not keen on anglers fishing flooded fields. Nor are employers, even if the angler struggles from his sickbed to work on Monday morning. He makes the place look so untidy as he sits huddled over the radiator, coughing and spluttering.

Undertakers, on the whole, are quite glad of the extra business.

Fishing Through the Ages

The First Recorded Gillies

A carving found in the ruins of ancient Thebes depicts an angler sitting in a chair and others lying on rugs spread on the ground, fishing from recumbent postures. Slaves were in attendance, taking care of such things as unhooking and rebaiting. Even in those days the well-britched could enjoy catching fish without ever having to handle the beastly things.

The Things They Said

Doing What Comes Naturally

> It is said that gardeners and fishermen make fine old men. This is not surprising. They have been caught up into Nature, grow old with a good will and no hanging back, and are without misgivings about their own mortality.
> *Conrad Voss Bark*

Remember that. Next time people call you a grumpy old bugger . . .

Traditional Angling Techniques

Screaming quietly as you float past the pub.

You have fallen in the river while attempting to fish the flooded fields, after ignoring the landlord's lunchtime warning that you were taking on board a little too much rocket fuel.

By now, he and his lady wife will be snug in the marital couch, taking a well-earned forty winks before opening again in the evening. You do not wish to disturb them by making too much commotion, but at the same time you would rather not drown. Messy for all concerned, and you've got your wage packet in your pocket.

Eek . . .

It's a Date

February 1

The salmon fishing season starts on the first day of February. Or it would if it hadn't already started or wasn't due to start yet. To put it another way, there are so many local variations to the start of the salmon fishing season that it's not really a date. Still, it's a nice thought.

February 2

Candlemas Day, February 2, is said to give a guide to the weather to come. Hope for a nasty wet day: if it's fine and frosty it means that there's more winter to come than we've had so far.

As the old Scots proverb puts it:

> *If Candlemas Day be dry and fair,*
> *The half o' winter's come and mair;*
> *If Candlemas Day be wet and foul,*
> *The half o' winter was gane at Youl.*

And what the hell that means, God only knows.

Know Your Fish

Bleak (*Alburnus alburnus*)

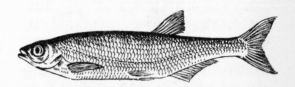

According to the book:
A small, silver fish that feeds in shoals near the surface. Often the saviour of matchmen, but otherwise seldom fished for seriously. Takes maggot on light float tackle.
Record: 4 oz 4 dms (0.12 kg)
Between ourselves:
A flaming nuisance, with a habit of pecking the float and decapitating maggots on the drop. Apart from matchmen and small boys, fished for only by the dastardly continentals. Can be got rid of, in theory, by throwing a crust in the stream which floats away and takes the shoal with it. Sod's Law decrees that the crust finds an eddy to circle round in, attracting dozens more bleak, a flock of ducks and – if your luck's really in – a convoy of swans.

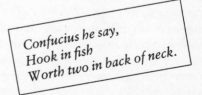

Confucius he say,
Hook in fish
Worth two in back of neck.

16

Salmon (*Salmo salar*)

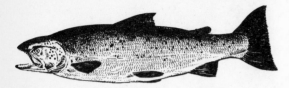

According to the book:
Big, noble, brave and beautiful. A splendid fighter. Returns from the sea to spawn in the same water it was hatched in, finding its way by smell. Caught on spinners or wet fly. Not averse to a string of lobworms, threaded up the line like a snake.
Record: 64 lb (29.029 kg)
Between ourselves:
Members of the bigger angling clubs can now fish some salmon waters quite cheaply. Best beats, however, are snapped up by syndicates for the use of tweedy twits and well-britched novices. The salmon would be appearing in greater numbers in cleaned-up rivers if it were not clobbered by commercial interests before it cleared the estuaries. It spends a great deal of time and energy getting to its spawning grounds. After which, its sex life must come as a great disappointment.

Zander (*Stizostedion lucioperca*)

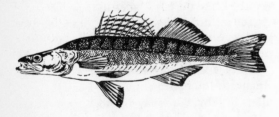

According to the book:
Sometimes known as the pike-perch, the zander is neither pike nor perch, but a completely separate imported fish. First introduced to Britain in 1878. Really established in 1960 when 500 fingerlings were put into the Great Ouse Relief Channel. Since then has spread rapidly.

Takes small, flashy lures and spun, wobbled or ledgered deadbaits. Best to use pike tackle with wire traces. The zander seems to like murky water and feeds best at dusk and dawn. Unpredictable scrapper. Some fight like pike, others throw in the towel early.
Record: 17 lb 4 oz (7.824 kg)
Between ourselves:
Best not to mention zander in a strange club unless you're sure what the policy is towards them. Many anglers love 'em. Others hate 'em to pieces for their habit of whopping into the roach and bream stocks. Taste nice, though. Zander, that is.

It's a Fact

Sunburned Salmon

Scientists have discovered the cause of ulcerated dermal necrosis – a nasty skin condition – in salmon. It's sunburn.

The salmon is safe enough in the sea, but gets sunburned as it swims up shallow estuaries and rivers to spawn.

There is a cure. But so far scientists have not found a way of slapping suntan lotion on the salmon as they come in from the sea. Not without losing a lot of scientists.

Glutton for Punishment

In February 1984 an angler caught the same pike three times in four hours on the River Stour, near Canterbury. And the 21 lb fish was the same one he'd caught in the same spot the year before. Which seems to indicate that the freshwater shark, for all its ferocity, is pretty stupid.

Knock, knock.
Who's there?
Sonia.
Sonia who?
Sonia tiddler. You said it was a whopper.

Know Your Tackle

The Reel

There are three main types of reel: the *centre pin*, the *fixed spool* and the *multiplier*.

Young anglers are encouraged by their fathers to start with the centre-pin – the basic wheel type of reel – on the grounds that it's the only way to learn; that when their prentice hands have mastered the centre-pin, then they are skilled enough to progress to the fixed spool. The real reason fathers insist on this is that the centre-pin is cheaper and it stops the little perishers catching more fish than they do.

The main attraction of the centre-pin is that, with the ratchet on, it makes much more noise than the fixed spool, thus advertising your prowess to other anglers. A generous sprinkling of sand in the works adds greatly to the effect.

The fixed spool was invented in 1905, and for forty or more years it was condemned as unsporting because it made long-distance casting far too easy. The protests came mainly from anglers who couldn't afford one.

Care should be taken, when threading the line through the rod rings, that the fixed-spool bale arm has been placed in the 'off' position. Failure to do this results in the line being on the wrong side to be picked up on the strike, which allows the fish to swim off unhindered and causes the angler to say a lot of naughty words.

The multiplier, used mainly for sea fishing or spinning, allows rapid reeling-in. The main value of this is that a hooked fish arrives at the net too dizzy to put up much of a fight, or that a predatory fish gets fed up failing to catch the speeding spinner and settles for a stationary deadbait.

Multipliers are prone to birds' nests on the cast, and so are invaluable to anyone learning proficiency in knots.

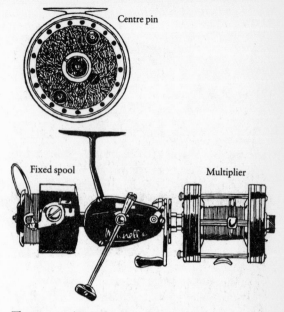

Three types of reel. The fixed spool and the multiplier have been stuck together because we thought they'd look prettier that way.

I Say, I Say, I Say . . .

The old Scottish laird wanted his dim son to do well on the ancestral salmon beat. So he bought him the finest rod and tackle money could buy, and sent him down to the river with the estate's oldest, most experienced and most trusted gillie. At the end of the day the boy and the gillie returned, and the laird called in the gillie.

'Tell me now, Angus,' he said, 'honestly and with no prevarication. How did the boy comport himself on the river today?'

'Marvellously, m'laird. Supairbly,' said Angus. 'If I may be permitted tae say so, even magnificently. But today Providence saw fit tae be mairciful tae the fish.'

'You're out of the club team,' said the captain. 'Out. Through. Finished.'

'Oh, yes,' said the disgruntled angler. 'And who do you suppose will be able to fill the gap?'

'Gap?' said the captain. 'I wasn't aware you'd be leaving one.'

A royal matchfisher at the South Yorkshire shore championships of 1030 AD complaining about misprints in the tide tables. The match secretary (grovelling) knows he's going to cop it at the next committee meeting.

Who Runs the Club?

The Freshwater Captain

The freshwater captain is in charge of the freshwater activities of the club. Until anyone fearless or daft enough to become match secretary can be found, his duties include the organisation of matches. He is the inland equivalent of the sea commodore (see August), but usually with two legs and no parrot.

His first duty is to maintain the waters in good condition, which means the organisation of regular working parties to cut undergrowth, clear weeded-up swims, shift silt and tidy up rubbish.

The organisation of a working party is simple enough, or it would be if he could find the people. At the very mention of the words, the bar empties. All that can be heard is the thunder of wellies as the members race home to their nearest and dearest.

In dozens of homes the same words are uttered by ever-loving wives: 'You're home early, pet. And sober. What is it – another working party?'

Among the qualities required of the freshwater captain are drive and enthusiasm. He realises why as he combs the pubs of the town looking for members lurking in dark corners. That's where the drive comes in. The enthusiasm is something he tries to pass on by lyrical descriptions of the benefits to be gained on a working party: fresh air, healthy exercise, companionship, the satisfaction of a job well done and a worthwhile water to fish in at the end of it.

Both drive and enthusiasm are sapped as he listens to plea after plea of previous engagements covering twenty-four hours of each day for the next six weeks; to heartrending accounts of rheumatism, lumbago, bad backs, bad fronts, double hernias, flat feet, rising arches, piles, halitosis, swine fever, beri-beri and terminal dandruff.

But persistence pays off and eventually he gets the blokes together, often by making them an offer they can't refuse, such as free booze.

He is responsible for providing the tools for the job, which include chainsaws, long-handled slashers and heavy-duty secateurs. He is then responsible for ensuring that members do not return home with bits of themselves missing through over-enthusiastic or cack-handed use of such tools. The toll of casualties can be minimised by providing the free booze *after* the job, not before or during. This also ensures that everyone stays to the end instead of sloping off after a couple of desultory slashes.

Should the club lack a fish recorder, the freshwater captain can make himself responsible for identifying doubtful or disputed species. If he can identify what appears to be a record roach as just a good-sized chub, he will prevent the club from looking silly. Not only that, he will save the captor a small fortune if the fish can be identified before he's bought drinks all round.

Stocking the waters is an important part of his duties, and stock control includes the discouragement of unauthorised importation of unwanted species into club waters. Any attempts by members to introduce zander, catfish, piranha or creatures from the Black Lagoon should be dealt with by firm methods such as suspension (preferably by the thumbs) or a swift kick to the naughty bits.

For stocking operations the captain usually gets a bigger turnout of helpers than he does for the working parties: the lads are keen to see what's going into their water. They stand on the bank after tipping the fish in, looking forward to the coming season in a fever of anticipation. The fish, meanwhile, are gliding gently downstream to settle in the waters belonging to the rival club.

Hints for Club Officials

The weigh-in should be conducted in an orderly fashion, and any attempts at deception severely dealt with. Women are best kept out of it.

Your Luck in the Stars

PISCES

Pisces (*February 20–March 20*)

Oo's a tiddly boy, then?

You are not physically robust, which is to say you are a right wimp. So by your birthday you are likely to be feeling the effects of February Filldyke: tiddly round the kiddleys and chilly round the willy.

This may cause you to spend less time on the bank and more time in the pub, if that's possible. Yours is a water sign, the sign of the fish, which gives you a deep and abiding interest in liquids, making it possible for you to be an industrial chemist, an oil tycoon or a drunk. You are probably not an industrial chemist or an oil tycoon.

Your fondness for liquids – a condition known in angling and astrological circles as *pisced* – could explain why you keep falling in the water. You put it down to an underdeveloped sense of direction brought about by your mind always being full of lofty thoughts. You're an *artiste*, you are, too preoccupied with aesthetic musings to notice that you're about to fall in the cut.

Yours is a highly sensitive sign, easily hurt by criticism or having a rod rest shoved up your nose. Rod rests are shoved up your nose quite frequently, as you are not above using aids to your match technique which do not meet with the approval of competitors or stewards.

Those fish in your deadly rival's stretch, for instance, floating belly-up. Looking for all the world as if they'd been affected by some toxic substance such as medicated shampoo. Nothing to do with you. Perhaps your deadly rival should wash his feet more often.

Those dead fish discovered down your wellies at the start of the match? They must have jumped in there and committed mass suicide as you walked along the bank. What other explanation could there be, for Pete's sake? And that mackerel you're weighing in? So? What's wrong with mackerel? Nothing, out at sea. Quite common, in fact. But a bit unusual on the Grand Union Canal.

You live in a world of fantasy and illusion. In other words, you lie a lot. What's more, you believe it yourself. Not only will you fib your way out of any trouble on the bank – or strain yourself in the pub trying to illustrate the size of the bait – you get very upset when others cast doubt upon your veracity.

You're not in trouble for very long, though: your gift of the gab and long-winded explanations mean that others back down in despair halfway through, finish up feeling rotten about having doubted you in the first place, and buy you a pint to restore your hurt feelings.

You daydream a lot, too, failing to notice that the float is bobbing wildly in the middle of your reverie. Which is why you seldom make a top-flight matchman and even get thrown out of the D-Team Third Reserves, known to other matchmen as Duffers' Dozen.

It is often claimed, by the more literally-minded astrologers, that you can tell Pisces people by their feet. They stand with their legs crossed in a fishlike manner (have you ever seen a fish with its legs crossed?). And there is a softness about their eyes (it says here) as if tears were waiting to flow.

Deeper research by the Parker Institute for the Study of Anglers' Aberrations has come up with the answer. A Piscean does indeed stand with his legs crossed. And there is definitely a watery look about his eyes. This has nothing to do with the Piscean's affinity with fish. But everything to do with the fact that he left the bank too late to answer a call of nature in a dignified fashion, and is now hopping up and down at the back of the queue in the nearest pub loo. His eyes are watering? Of course his eyes are watering. Wouldn't yours?

Most Pisceans are secretive and indecisive. They're secretive, anyway, but often can't make up their minds whether or not they're indecisive. And the sign of the two fish, heading in different directions, means that often you don't know whether you're coming or going. The secrecy means that nobody's going to get any jealously guarded tips for bait or technique out of you. Not that you have any for long: you try a different bait every week and most times, like as not, forget to take them down to the water.

The secretiveness and indecision, plus the fondness for liquids, often leads to friction with loved ones. They're not easy traits to live with and a spouse may resort to nagging when a Piscean arrives home late, falling about and fibbing. This leads to the stereotyped situation of Pisces being driven to drink. Not that he ever needs much driving.

All in all, being a Piscean can be quite enjoyable. Once you get used to being misunderstood.

It's a Fact

Cut Up About It

In February 1980 a Welsh angler sold a fish he'd caught to a motel, thinking it was a salmon. The motel manager spotted that the fish, which had been cut into twenty-five portions, was a brown trout. When it was put back together again it weighed 21 lb, well over the British record of 19 lb 9¼ oz.

Even more upset about the fate of his catch was American angler Billy Johnson, who in April 1982 caught a largemouth bass weighing more than 23 lb. His wife cooked the fish and the family ate it. It was delicious.

Billy lost his appetite when he discovered that the bass was a world record and would have been worth £500,000 in endorsements and promotions.

Great Angling Inventions

The Pongerblonger

Designed to cut down the incidence of asphyxiation among anglers' nearest and dearest when washing out any long johns or lucky socks. Also recommended for wear around the house when the master is at home, in case he takes his wellies off suddenly and without warning.

Knock, knock.
Who's there?
Ida.
Ida who?
Ida bite just then.

Fishing Through The Ages

Naughty Yorkies

Match angling, tradition has it, started in Sheffield in the mid nineteenth century. Fishing in the industrial North of England was badly hit by pollution; if there were fish in the waters at all, they were sickly and stunted. So the Sheffield cutlers and grinders went down to the nearest river on Sundays, pegged out the bank and fished a given time for a prize, usually a copper kettle.

A famous angler of the time, J. W. Martin, attended one of these matches and was not at all impressed with what he saw. Even less by what he heard:

> This particular match had only about fifty contestants, but they must have been selected from the very scum of the Sheffield dregs. They were, I was informed, a party of the very lowest of the low grinders, men whose every word was an oath, men who exchanged compliments so painful and free that I thought would blister the tongues of those uttering them.
>
> These men had consumed more beer than was good for them ... Every now and then, one of the competitors would yell at the top of his voice to another 50 yards away to enquire in forcible language if he had 'copped owt yet?' and that one would reply in still more forcible terms: 'Ave I –!' First one, then another, more lucky than their fellows, managed to land a gudgeon or an infantile roach, and these feats were greeted with yells of derision ...

It couldn't happen these days. Could it?

Knock, knock.
Who's there?
Rhoda.
Rhoda who?
You Rhoda boat; I'll look after da beer.

Angling's Big Questions

Is Angling Cruel?

The question of whether fishing involves cruelty is constantly being raised and hotly argued on both sides.

Is it cruel? The answer, regrettably, has to be 'Yes'. Consider what is involved:

INTENSE physical exertion occasioned by the struggle against the hook, often leading to muscle strain and total exhaustion.

PAIN and damage caused during unhooking operations.

HOURS spent in an alien environment, resulting in tension and stress which can lead to emotional trauma and have an adverse effect on the heart.

UNACCUSTOMED exposure to the sun's rays, causing pain and damage to the skin.

DISRUPTION of normal feeding habits, resulting in stomach pains and digestive upsets.

EXPOSURE to infection from viruses and bacteria not encountered in the normal environment.

PHYSICAL damage caused by jostling, rough handling and careless transportation.

EXPOSURE to extremes of temperature.

SEVERE dehydration, which has an unsettling effect on the metabolism.

Yes, there's no doubt about it. The angler suffers terribly. The fish, on the other hand . . .

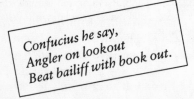

Confucius he say,
Angler on lookout
Beat bailiff with book out.

Knock, knock.
Who's there?
Ivor.
Ivor who?
Ivor big 'un on.

I Say, I Say, I Say . . .

The lovely young girl was walking by the river on a hot Summer's day when finally she couldn't resist the lure of the cool, clear water. She left all her clothes on the bank, dived in and floated blissfully downriver.

Awakened from her reverie by a long, low whistle, she opened her eyes to see an angler staring at her. Her clothes were by now a long way behind. As she was wondering what to do, she spotted an old tin bath in the shallows. Picking it up, she held it in front of her and walked out of the water.

'You dirty old man!' she shouted at the angler. 'You know what I think —'

'Yes, love,' said the angler. 'You think that bath's got a bottom in it.'

Did you hear about the scientist who crossed an octopus with a wire coat hanger and got an eight-boom paternoster?

There was an argument among the customers of the posh saloon bar of a riverside pub: 'Which smells worse — a goat or a coarse fisherman?'

To settle it, they brought a goat into the saloon. When they'd stopped coughing, they asked an angler from the public bar to join them for a drink. The angler walked happily into the saloon — and the goat fainted.

The Angler's Guide to March

For the coarse angler, March is a cruel month.

There are the notorious March winds, for a start, scourge of the reservoir fisherman who follows the experts' advice about fishing into the wind and the reason why few March anglers go fishing in a kilt.

Anglers whose noses or ears drop off as a result of prolonged exposure are advised not to panic, but to place the appendage in a clean plastic bag and take it to the nearest casualty ward. They can do wonders with replacement surgery these days. Anglers with a broken or otherwise misshapen nose should ensure that the surgeon knows which way up it ought to be. A nose replaced upside down means that every time you sneeze your cap blows off.

Ears replaced back to front are not so serious a problem: at least you'll know when your deadly rivals are talking about you behind your back.

The cruellest thing of all about March is that the fifteenth sees the start of the three-month close season for coarse fish. Except, that is, in Yorkshire, where it started on February 28. And in Devon and Cornwall, where there is no close season. There is no close season, either, in the Lincolnshire Division stillwaters of the Anglian Water Authority. Nor in Eire. Nor over much of Scotland, where usually only the game fish close seasons are observed. Not that the Scots in the main seem even to have heard of coarse fish. Vermin, they are. (The fish, not the Scots.) Incidentally, there's no Sunday fishing in Scotland.

Many areas in the British Isles have no close season for eels. So that's something you could try for. And if the odd perch grabs at your lobworm, how the heck were you to stop it?

So perhaps it's not so much cruel as highly confusing. And perhaps the best advice to any frustrated coarse fisherman is 'On yer bike'.

March 1 sees the opening of the trout season (except for rainbow trout, whose season starts on May 16, mostly, but varies from area to area). So any coarse angler really suffering withdrawal symptoms could put aside his prejudices and join the game fishermen for a while.

He could start with still-water trout fishing, preferably on a newly-stocked water where the hand-reared trout have not had time to become suspicious, thinking that every weighted lure is another high-protein pellet. (What was that about prejudices?) Once he's got the hang of things he could move on to chasing wild brownies in fast water.

Now and again he'll run into the tweedy-twit type of game fisher who thinks that coarse fishing is only one step removed from glue sniffing, certainly not a pastime for an officer and a gentleman. It's really only ignorance on their part, and any remarks such as, 'Coarse fisherman, eh? *Extremely* coarse, I'd say,' can be countered by a sophisticated riposte such as a swift welly to the naughty bits.

(Only kidding. Ha ha. We don't want to give coarse anglers a bad name, do we?)

Things You Can Do to Take Your Mind off the Close Season

1. Dispose of surplus bait. Put the worms back on the compost heap. DON'T put the sausages back in the freezer.
2. Exterminate surplus maggots. If you leave them in the tins, you're in for a nasty shock in a couple of weeks' time.
3. Take up game fishing.
4. Take up sea fishing.
5. Take up drink/sex/gambling/mugging old ladies/kicking the cat.
6. In cases of severe withdrawal symptoms, take up gardening, decorating or do-it-yourself. But make sure you make a hell of a mess of it.
7. Join the Foreign Legion (La Légion Etrangère, La Citadelle, Lille. Tel: 51-92-00).
8. Catch the first boat to Ireland. No close season there (see March 17, p. 26). Why didn't you think of that in the first place?

Traditional Angling Techniques

Getting a whopper close to the bank and then remembering you've forgotten to make up the landing net.

It's a Date

March 1

March 1, as well as being the first day of the trout fishing season, is also the Welsh national day, celebrating the patron saint, Dewi Sant or St David.

In the sixth century St David was abbot-bishop of a monastery in St David's, Dyfed. Monasteries being dependent on fish at least one day a week, and St David's being where it is, St David was almost certainly skilled in the arts of trout fishing and sea fishing.

He was known to his followers, in fact, as 'The Waterman', which could have been a tribute to his boating and fishing skills. Another and less appealing theory is that he and his monks were teetotallers.

This certainly does not apply to the average Welshman on St David's Day. Anyone wandering the bank sporting a leek or daffodil in his buttonhole, singing rugby songs while balancing a pint pot on his head, and falling in the water with a loud cry of 'Cymru am byth!' is likely to be a Welshman. Just hope he keeps away from your swim.

March 14

Last day of the coarse fishing season in most areas of England and Wales.

Towards midnight there is a sharp rise in the incidence of fibbing, falling in the water, alcohol poisoning, wife-beating and husband-battering. Mothers-in-law are insulted profusely and cats kicked unmercifully. Sometimes cats are insulted profusely and mothers-in-law kicked unmercifully. RSPCA on standby. Police leave cancelled and magistrates' courts put on red alert.

March 15

First day of the coarse fishing close season in most parts of England and Wales.

On 15 March, 44 BC, Julius Caesar was assassinated. It wasn't a good day for him, either.

March 17

For those of you who caught the first boat to Ireland – sorry about that. St Patrick's Day on March 17 is a great day for the Irish and a very jolly occasion, but you are unlikely to get much fishing done, even if you can find anyone sober enough to sell you the bait.

Stick a shamrock in your buttonhole, a shillelagh under your arm, and join in the fun. If anyone asks your religion, say you're Buddhist. You'll get thumped for that as well. Just remember, it's nothing personal.

Now, me bucko, what are yez afther havin'?

Mother's Day

Mothering Sunday is the fourth Sunday in Lent, which puts it around the middle of March.

Make sure the kids buy their mother something really useful: a set of floats, a reel, a new spinning rod, bottle of Scotch.

Make your contribution by not sitting around bewailing the end of the coarse season. Make yourself useful by doing a few little jobs around the house. Or just clear off to the shed to get from under her feet.

March 21

March 21 is the first day of Spring. Not that the coarse angler takes any notice. He's sunk deep in close-season dooms.

The sap is rising. The little lambs are gambolling. The daffodils are swaying in the breeze. The catkins dangle from the boughs. The buds are bursting. And the birds are singing merrily.

Who the hell wants to know about soppy stuff like that when there's no decent fishing for three months?

Spring?

Bah!

Humbug!

Know Your Fish

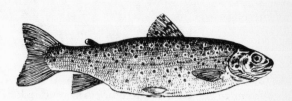

Trout

According to the book:
Game, hard-fighting fish. The brown trout (*Salmo trutta*) is the only native British trout, despite all the local names which would appear to indicate different species. The sea trout is also a *Salmo trutta*, but with migratory habits. Introduced species of trout include the American brook trout (*Salvelinus fontinalis*) and the rainbow trout (*Salmo gairdneri*).

Records: Brown trout 19 lb 9 oz 4 dms (8.880 kg); Sea trout 20 lb (9.071 kg); American brook trout 5 lb 13 oz 8 dms (2.65 kg); Rainbow trout 19 lb 8 oz (8.844 kg).

Between ourselves:
Still-water stocking has introduced many more anglers than ever before to trout fishing, though with hand-reared trout used to having buckets of high-protein pellets chucked at them for din-dins, it's not quite the challenge offered by fishing for wild trout. In certain quarters, trout fishing techniques are still hampered by old-fashioned snobbery (dray flay and all that), but there's not so much as there used to be. For all the mystique surrounding the trout, it's still one of the dimmest fish that swims.

Knock, knock.
Who's there?
Don.
Don who?
Don just stand there – pass the landing net.

Know Your Tackle

The Landing Net

This comes basically in two pieces, the net and the handle, and is used to net the fish as it is drawn on the line to the bank. The golden rule is to make up the landing net before anything else; before you even assemble the rod.

Many anglers, in their hurry to get to the fish, neglect to do this, and find themselves with the catch of the season on the line and the landing net lying in two pieces at the top of the bank. Assuming, that is, that it's been unpacked at all.

Those who do make up the net tend to forget it in their wanderings and hook a whopper 50 yards round the river bend.

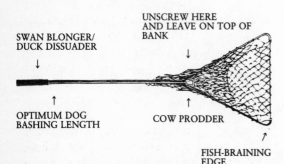

A landing net and things you can do with it.

Those who keep the net constantly by their side can also suffer from the application of Sod's Law when the bottom of the net – which has frayed a little and which they have been meaning to mend for weeks – gives way under the weight of the first decent fish.

The handle gets far more use than the net as a cow-prodder, swan-blonger, duck-dissuader and dog-basher. A telescopic handle allows cows to be prodded, swans to be blonged and ducks dissuaded at some distance from the bank; dogs can be bashed well before they can steal your butties, sneeze in your maggots or cock their legs up against your basket.

When landing a fish, the idea is to have the net in the water before the fish gets to the bank and then to draw the fish gently over the rim, dropping the rod tip as the net is lifted clear of the water.

Why so many anglers wait until the fish is thrashing almost at their feet and then brain it with the net, causing it to jerk and break the line, is one of the deeper mysteries of angling.

I Say, I Say, I Say . . .

A man approached the angler on the bank and asked, 'Any luck?'

'Nothing today so far,' said the angler. 'But yesterday I couldn't go wrong. Caught forty-five massive trout from this very spot.'

'Really?' said the stranger. 'How interesting. Do you know who I am?'

'No.'

'I'm the local magistrate, chairman of the Water Authority, and just happen to own this stretch of private water.'

'Oh dear,' said the angler. 'Do you know who I am?'

'No.'

'The biggest bloody liar for miles.'

Knock, knock.
Who's there?
Butcher.
Butcher who?
Butcher hand in your pocket – it's your round.

Knock, knock.
Who's there?
Aldus.
Aldus who?
Aldus who aren't fishing – kindly leave the bank.

Knock, knock.
Who's there?
Martin.
Martin who?
Martin of maggots has fallen in the cut.

Who Runs the Club?

The Match Secretary

The match secretary looks after the organisation of the club's matches. Let's face it, with a title like that you wouldn't expect him to do anything else.

It sounds like the ideal job for the club's ace matchman; at least he knows what match fishing is all about. But he would find his style more than cramped: with all the organisation, paperwork, keeping order on the bank, he wouldn't have much time left for fishing. The job's better going to someone who enjoys organising, whether or not he knows one end of a fish from another.

Anyway, that's basically what the match secretary does: plans a programme of matches through the season, ensures that all permissions and permits are acquired, and sees that everything goes smoothly on the day.

He should be especially careful to ensure that Water Authority rod licences have been bought, or are available. To turn up on a Sunday morning without licences, to find that the bailiff does not sell them, that all the tackle shops are shut, and that the pubs are not open for another five hours, can lead to some diminution of members' confidence in the match secretary, sometimes demonstrated by throwing him in the water or filling his Y-fronts with starving maggots.

The same goes for checking, a few days before, that the water is still available; that it's not been double-booked, that it's not flooded or polluted, and even that it's still there. A break in the bank, an accident to the lock gates, over-enthusiastic clearing or dredging, or a prolonged dry spell could mean that all the members have to fish in is a stretch of mud. Again, the members are not well pleased. And a mob of highly dischuffed anglers is not a pretty sight.

The match secretary is responsible for the appointment of stewards to supervise the contest. These should be chosen for their tact and diplomacy as well as for their forcefulness or strength of character. Applications from bovver boys, football hooligans, club bouncers, kung-fu experts, former members of the Mafia, SS or Gestapo, should be treated warily, as should those from members known to take their responsibilities too seriously. A match which ends up with everyone disqualified and the bank littered with broken bodies is not likely to be voted The Most Enjoyable Event of the Year.

The more muscular of the stewards can be used to supervise the peg draw and the weigh-in, neither operation noted for its orderliness. Two or more stewards at the weigh-in, each watching out for particular transgressions of the rules, helps to stop the application of such aids to success as:

Double entries of sizeable fish;
Thumbs on the scale basket;
Twiddling the dial adjustment knob;
Slipping in the odd half brick;
Entry of fish which obviously departed this
    life well before the match;
Fish which are suspiciously heavy for their
    size, perhaps on account of the spiral
    leads they unaccountably swallowed.

The match secretary should make an abbreviated note of each catch in a special notebook – 2r, 6g, 3p: 1.15. Which means 2 roach, 6 gudgeon, 3 perch: 1 lb 15 oz. (Nowadays you're supposed to record the weights also in kilogrammes and things, but that's better left until you get home. You've got enough problems as it is.)

The reason for the notebook is so that you can write up the results later in the official record book, so saving it from becoming soiled on the bank. The notebook is a most valuable document; until the entries are written up, it's the only record of the day's activities. Which makes all the more strange the number which are left behind, turning soggy on damp pub counters, at the end of the night.

Hard as it may be, the match secretary should not fish in the events he organises. There's enough to do as the match wears on, for one thing. For another, if he draws a good peg he'll spend the next half hour defending himself against cries of 'Fiddle!', 'Swizz!', 'Carve-up!', 'How come you got that peg and I've got Gudgeons' Graveyard again?'

Nor should he involve himself in the pegging-out. His presence is needed at the match HQ to check in arriving anglers. He may also be needed to calm down the local bailiff who is demanding to know where all these roughnecks have come from and who said they could park on his front lawn?

After the weigh-in, the lads will be keen to be off, especially if they're travelling by coach. The driver will have arrived bang on time, on pain of slow death or sudden mutilation, and will have been intensively briefed about which pub is the first port of call.

But first the match secretary must ensure that all the pegs have been recovered and all the litter collected from the bank. (At this point he discovers why trying to organise working parties has sent the match captain round the bend.) Before he leaves the water he must thoroughly clean the scales, especially if he is taking them home.

Even at the most careful weigh-in, the scales get covered with an incredible amount of fish slime, which doesn't take too long to start to pong. Fifty per cent of divorces among match secretaries are attributable to the good lady wife's worrying about the smell on the landing, tearing the place apart in an attempt to locate it, and finally calling in the sanitary man who tracks down the uncleaned scales in the cupboard under the stairs.

Hints for Club Officials

Always ensure that your booking of a water does not clash with that of another club.

Your Luck in the Stars

Aries (*March 21–April 20*)

Have mouth, will travel

The original Action Man, you are. Never still for a minute, always charging off in different directions. So we're not likely to find you sitting by the water in the rain, patiently waiting for your float to dip. You're roaming the bank with spinner or fly, searching out one likely spot after another.

You're the leader, the pioneer, the discoverer of all the hotspots. Next day, thanks to your great big mouth, you'll find them crammed with other anglers so you'll be off on the move again.

Whatever else you do, you've got to catch something. The fact that your nickname in the club is Bighead suggests that your ego is not exactly underdeveloped. You need constant praise and recognition, so you go all out to have something to boast about at the club and back home. Though you're normally honest, you're not above buying a couple of trout at the fishmonger's after a fruitless day. You salve your conscience by asking the fishmonger to throw the trout to you across the counter. Then you can go home and truthfully say you caught 'em.

You can be a great driving force in the club, if it's only driving fellow members round the bend, but you're better acting as a one-man ginger group than taking a position of responsibility. Details bore you, and you've not got the patience to sit through a committee meeting. Half an hour of listening to waffle and

you're missing, sinking a couple of pints in the pub next door.

You're not keen on authority, nor cowed by officialdom. So you're the bloke to tell the secretary he's a bumbling old twit, and to tell the officious bailiff where to put his rule book.

A great champion of the underdog, you go to the aid of the little feller who's being turfed out of a productive swim by a burly bloke with a broken nose. As you're waiting for the ambulance, you discover that the big bloke really had baited up the swim the night before and that the little feller – probably Pisces – is notorious for pinching other people's swims.

One way or the other, you often return from a fishing trip the worse for wear. If you've not been thumped for outspokenness, you've generally fallen over something, off something or into something. You're the most accident-prone sign of the zodiac, worse even than Sagittarius, and vulnerable in the head, face and knees.

Afraid of nothing, you wade deeper than is safe, or leap from rock to rock in midstream, failing to notice all that slippery weed. You're the one on beach or pier who walks behind another angler just as he's into his backswing with a 4oz lead.

Fearless though you are, you can't stand pain. The slightest bump or scratch will have you hopping about and screaming for a doctor, or at the very least a stretcher to the pub for a large Scotch.

The large Scotch, plus a few soothing words from your mates, soon helps you forget the pain, but it sets you up immediately for another dose of trouble. One large Scotch leads naturally to another, and too many of them help to trigger off your fiery temper. That's not difficult because you can't stand criticism. When it's suggested that perhaps you were a bit of a Silly Billy, trying to jump the gap on the opening lock gates, you are very likely to explode. And once you've exploded you're likely to get thumped again.

You have an engaging manner and an ability to hold forth on subjects you know absolutely nothing about. So you'll quite happily give the club's champion matchman a half-hour lecture on bleak-bashing. Because of your sensitivity to criticism you can be upset again. Not because you've been told to shut up, but because your listener has implied that his interest is waning by stuffing cotton wool in his ears, falling to sleep or sucking a scampi-flavoured cyanide pill.

You have a springy, athletic walk and, because of the time you spend in the open air, a healthy tan. These are useful assets in your other pursuit – women. You have a tremendous appetite for sex and are able to keep several romances on the go at the same time, even to the extent of letting them interfere with your fishing.

The great thing is to ensure that all your loved ones do not turn up at the club's annual prize-giving to see you receive the award for *The Member Most Likely To*. Not only is it embarrassing if they interrupt the ceremony by fighting over you, it doesn't go down too well with the wife.

The Things They Said

The Gentle Touch

> Sir Henry Wotton . . . was also a most dear lover, and a frequent practiser of the art of angling; of which he would say, 'it was an employment for his idle time, which was then not idly spent . . . a rest to his mind, a cheerer of his spirits, a diverter of sadness, a calmer of unquiet thoughts, a moderator of passions, a procurer of contentedness; and that it begat habits of peace and patience in those that professed and practised it.
>
> *Izaak Walton (1593–1683)*
> *The Compleat Angler*

That's what the man said, anyway. If you finish the day in a foul temper, thoroughly miserable, soaked to the skin, dying for a pint and just in the mood to kick hell out of the cat, perhaps you're not doing it right. You and 4,000,000 others.

It's a Fact

Keep Going, You Fool . . .

A brown trout's heartbeat is slow and regular, approaching its maximum rate only 1 per cent of the time. Because 1 square metre of river bottom contains enough food to keep a trout for a week, the fish spends most of its time stationary.

If a trout is removed from its regular swim and put back in a strange part of the river, it gets into a state of anxiety and its heart races until it finds its way 'home' again.

Sometimes a trout's heart will miss a beat – when a shadow passes over the water or when a fly is cast above it.

Some Side-Splitting End-of-Season Jokes

Some anglers give up the chance of the last day's fishing for health reasons. Their wives threaten to kill them if they go.

The Sludgethorpe Waltonians lost every match of the season.

'Never mind, eh?' said a supporter as the team left the canal with not a fish to its name. 'At least our lads are good losers.'

'Good?' said the captain. 'Good? They're bloody perfect!'

On the way from the water the supporter came across one of the matchmen belabouring a little boy.

'Just a minute,' he said. 'Why are you knocking that little lad about?'

'We've lost every match, haven't we?'

'So?'

'So, he's our mascot.'

Great Angling Inventions

The Pedal-Yourself Bottomless Dinghy

For boat anglers of limited means who don't mind getting wet.

Don't Forget to Write . . .

Straight To The Top

Communication with the club patron (see December), especially if he is of high rank, should be respectful and formal, i.e. obsequious, fawning, grovelling and pompous. It does him no harm to be kept in touch with the club's activities through short progress reports, even though he won't have the faintest idea what you're wittering on about. (The letter should, of course, be written by the club secretary.)

The end of the season is an appropriate time for such a report, perhaps combined with the invitation for him to attend and officiate at the annual prize-giving dinner and dance.

> The Earl of Sludgethorpe,
> Sludgethorpe Manor,
> Sludgethorpe Heights,
> Sludgethorpe.
>
> My Lord,
> On behalf of the committee, officials and members of Sludgethorpe Waltonians, I am writing to ask if you would honour us again with your presence, and that of your good lady wife, at our annual end-of-season prize-giving dinner and dance.
>
> We should be honoured also if you would be so kind as to perform the prize-giving ceremony and to say a few words once more as our patron.
>
> This year the catering has been entrusted to an establishment of long standing and high repute, so there should be no recurrence of the digestive upsets which afflicted yourself and your lady wife after last year's function.
>
> Those members who last year so rudely interrupted your speech and threw bread rolls have since been expelled from the club, so there should be no repeat either of that unfortunate occurrence. They were widely believed to be infiltrators from Slagville Piscatorials who, as you know, are our rival club and whose methods of competition leave a lot to be desired.
>
> As your estate manager will confirm, the conduct of our members fishing your grounds this past season has been excellent. There have been the inevitable cases of falling in the water, but certainly no evidence of the pig-chasing or bullock-baiting which marred the previous season. The ducks which disappeared so mysteriously at Christmas are believed by our wildlife consultant to have been seized by a freak migratory urge.
>
> I trust you will find our invitation acceptable, and we all look forward to seeing yourself and your lady wife at our little function.
> I remain,
> Your obedient servant,
> Eli Witherspoon,
> Secretary, Sludgethorpe Waltonians Angling Club
> RSVP

I Say, I Say, I Say . . .

Prosecuting counsel (to angler accused of spearing an aggressive dog with the end of his rod): 'When the dog approached you, had you the butt of the rod over your shoulder?'

Angler: 'Yes, sir.'

Counsel: 'Then why did you not take the butt to him instead of the point?'

Angler: 'I would have done, sir, if the dog had taken its butt to me.'

Husband, back from a seven-day fishing festival: 'How did you feel while I was away, darling? I bet you missed me.'

Wife: 'Oh, no. Every night I took out some of your old fishing clothes and draped them all over the floor. I left a wet landing net in the kitchen and a slimy keepnet in the hall. I filled the ashtray with smelly old cigarette ends. Then I went out in the garden, came back in and trampled mud all over the carpets. It was just as if you'd never been away.'

'What time did you get home last night?' demanded the angler's wife.

'I must admit, my love,' he said, 'that it was a little after dark.'

'After dark! It was daylight when you got home!'

'So? Isn't that after dark?'

It's a Fact

Bouncing Billy

A Manchester man, Billy Barker, could leap across a canal in two jumps. Jump One took him to the middle, where his feet went just under the surface of the water. Jump Two took him safely to the other side. Just to prove it wasn't a fluke, he would do the same jump backwards.

His secret, apart from his superb physical fitness, was the fact that he held a 25 lb weight in each hand. The weights gave him the impetus he needed for the second jump.

Billy died in March 1965 at the age of eighty-four. Peacefully and nowhere near a canal. Which is more than you can say for some, especially those anglers who try to emulate his feat, 100 per cent of whom fail to reach the other side. The motivation comes from:

(a) Trying to reach the pub before it shuts.
(b) Leaving the pub long after it was supposed to shut.
(c) Elation at winning a match.
(d) Trying to evade pursuit after being caught fiddling a match.
(e) Trying to impress the match team's groupies.

Those who attempt the feat are known to their more polite friends as Silly Billies. To their less polite friends as Barmy Buggers.

I Say, I Say, I Say . . .

In his excitement at hooking a big fish, the angler fell off the end of the pier into the sea.

'Help!' he screamed. 'I can't swim! I can't swim!'

A drunk stuck his head over the rail. 'So what?' he said. 'I can't play the violin, but I don't go round shouting about it.'

It's a Fact

Happy Birthday

European freshwater eels have lived up to 90 years in captivity, and have even made it to 50 in the wild.

Fishing Jokes Not to Tell in Ireland on St Patrick's Day (or any day, come to that)

An English angler fishing in Ireland got on a bus and asked a local passenger if he could tell him where to get off for the river.

'Just keep your eye on me,' said the Irishman. 'And get off the stop before I do.'

There were the Irish anglers who drowned trying to push-start a motorboat.

And the ones who had a marvellous fishing trip. No fish, but they got £95 back on the empties.

Two Irish anglers hit trouble when the sail blew off their boat way out at sea.

'Don't worry, Patrick,' said one. 'We can use the engine.'

'The hell we can,' said Patrick. 'How do we get a thing that size to the top of the mast?'

Sign in a country lane by the Liffey: *When you can't see this notice, the road is under water.*

An Irish gillie was steering the boat through some very nasty rapids. 'Don't worry, sorr,' he shouted to the pale-faced English angler clinging to the thwarts. 'I know every rock on this river, so I do.'

There was a horrible ripping sound, a gaping hole appeared in the boat and gallons of water rushed in.

'Good God, man!' screamed the angler. 'I thought you said you knew every rock on this river!'

'So I do, sorr, so I do,' said the gillie. 'That's one of the big ones.'

The Angler's Guide to April

April is a funny month. Funny peculiar and funny ha-ha.

The fly fisherman is happy enough as the season settles into some kind of pattern for him, and his trusty wrist action is getting the fly where he wants it. More or less.

The fly hatches may be still not too predictable or plentiful, but they're happening. And if he's really not having the luck, he can always try for a few tame trout at the newly-stocked waters just to keep his hand in.

For the coarse fisherman, it's unsettling. He's either doing nothing at all, or fishing an area with no close season, or trying some sea fishing. But there's a sense of not belonging, of dispersion, a scattering of the old gang, a loss of the old comradeship, and a feeling of unfamiliarity about the new venues.

April 1, of course, is time for the traditional April Fool jokes, which are probably helped along by the general feeling of boredom or restlessness. There's one angling April Fool joke which is reported as gospel every year; it's obviously an apocryphal story, but it must have happened at some time.

It's about two sea anglers. One loses his false teeth, along with his breakfast, over the side of the boat.

His mate, for a lark, ties his own false teeth to the line and pretends to catch them.

'Hey!' he shouts to his mate. 'I've hooked your teeth.'

'Great!' says his mate. 'Give 'em here!'

He tries the teeth and finds they don't fit.

'These aren't my teeth,' he says. And chucks them over the side.

Leaving his mate speechless. And toothless.

To be serious. April is as good a time as any to start a wormarium, if you haven't already got one. (You can call it a wormery if you like, but wormarium sounds much more scientific: impresses the neighbours if not the wife.)

Dig over a small patch of unwanted or unproductive garden, and on it place a bottomless wooden box. Water the area inside the box well, and dig in plenty of damp, shredded paper. Throw on your old tea leaves, coffee grounds, sour milk and vegetable peelings. Almost anything organic will help: leaf-mould, straw, grass cuttings, dead pussycats, redundant mothers-in-law.

Every couple of inches, cover with a thin layer of soil: as well as helping the texture, it helps to neutralise any incipient pong.

Keep the wormarium moist and cover it with a sack. All you have to do then is keep adding the waste. By the time the coarse season starts, you'll have more worms than you can use. They won't be all that tough, mind you: living has been too easy. So they'll need scouring through moss for a few days before you use them. (Don't forget to turn the container upside-down every twenty-four hours.)

Incidentally, if you haven't got a garden or can't spare the ground, you can try the same thing in an old stone sink, or in a tub or box with holes in the bottom.

Some More Things You Can Do to Take Your Mind Off the Close Season

1. Ring the Samaritans.
2. Play with your floats.
3. Dismantle your reel for cleaning.
4. Take the bits of reel back to the shop to see if the man can put them together again.
5. Check your basket for:
    Mouldering butties
    Bits of cheese
    Empty Scotch bottles
    Full Scotch bottles (chance would be a fine thing)
    Fag packets with two left in
    Tights, knickers and bras
    Dead ducks
6. Introduce yourself to the kids.
7. Take the kids to the psychotherapist.

It's a Date

April 1

April 1 is, of course, All Fools' Day. If you're lucky enough to be fishing in what is normally the off-season for coarse fish, you've got all the gear to hand for some jolly pranks and ripping wheezes.

Among the things you can do to your mate as an April Fool jape are putting:
    Curry powder in his groundbait
    Soap in his swim
    Casters in his tobacco pouch
    Maggots in his butties
    Worms down his neck
    Pike down his trousers

. . . All of which are pretty silly things to do, but that's what April Fool jokes are all about. Your mate is bound to enter the spirit of the thing, perhaps to the extent of playing a little prank on you by way of retaliation. Such as knocking your silly teeth down your throat.

Traditional Angling Techniques

Doing something very nasty to a dog which has stolen your butties and peed up your leg.

It's a Fact

A Frog In Your Throat

Among the more revolting eating contests, which the respectable record books now eschew, is frog-swallowing.

A test case in Britain in the mid Seventies saw a local character, Poddy the Poacher, hauled up before Market Drayton magistrates accused of cruelty to frogs by swallowing them.

Poddy – who appeared in court dressed in a frogman's suit and flippers, with feathers in his hair – was in training for his attempt on the then record of five frogs in sixty-five seconds held by an Irishman called McNamara.

(Mind you, both Poddy and McNamara would have a long way to go to beat an international professional swallower, Mac Norton – known as The Human Aquarium – who downed three gallons of water and two dozen live frogs in one go.)

Poddy explained that he didn't actually *eat* the frogs; he washed them straight down with swigs of Guinness. After his solicitor claimed that swallowing frogs was no more cruel than using them as livebait for pike, Poddy was cleared and flip-flopped from the court without a stain on his wetsuit.

A live minnow-eating contest is held every year in Geraardsbergen, in Belgium. Like the frog-swallowing, it's more drinking than eating. The minnows are put in a large glass of red wine and slurped down.

A short-lived April Fool craze among British anglers was the practical joke of goldfish-eating. The angler would walk into a pub containing a fish tank, swish his hand around in the water, produce what appeared to be a goldfish and chomp it down in front of the horrified customers. The 'goldfish' was actually a piece of carrot which the angler had palmed as he walked in.

The jolly jape was discontinued after several anglers were beaten up by goldfish-lovers.

Sometimes, though, the fish gets its own back. A highly esteemed delicacy in Japan is the fu-gu fish. The one snag is that it is highly poisonous and has to be prepared by master chefs who know exactly what bits are what. Some restaurants obviously can't afford cooks of this calibre because two hundred Japanese die every year after tucking into the fu-gu.

'Ah, so. Derricious. Compriments to the – Aaaarrrrgh!'

Know Your Tackle

The Keepnet

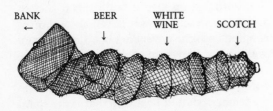

BANK   BEER   WHITE WINE   SCOTCH

Even distribution of essentials in a keepnet. Red wine and methylated spirits are best kept on the bank and served at air temperature. Any space left can be filled with fish, should you be so lucky.

This should be fully extended, propped open and staked out at both ends in a gentle current in the shade. If there's no shade, cover it with leafy twigs. This ensures that the cans and bottles of beer placed inside are kept properly cool, which is the keepnet's main function.

It is also used to keep fish alive and undisturbed until the end of the session when the catch can be counted, weighed and returned carefully to the water. What happens in practice is that the net is lifted out for a count and a drool every time a new fish is added to the total. Fish get very cheesed off with this and often express their disapproval by conking out.

Fish should be removed from the net at the end of the day, one by one, and placed gently back in the water facing upstream, so that the gills get a good supply of aerated water. Fish which appear to be distressed should be 'walked' upstream until they show signs of recovery.

Anglers often neglect to do this and keep the fish on the bank to drool over or photograph before slinging it back. Or, in their hurry to get to the boozer, just up-end the net and pour the lot back willy nilly. Either way is very naughty.

When the net is empty it should be washed to get rid of mud, slime, weed and scales before the journey home. Many of the objections by pub landlords to the presence of anglers can be attributed to their standing at the bar festooned with wet and smelly nets.

When the angler arrives home, the net should again be rinsed out in clean water and hung on the washing line to dry. The usual practice is to bung it unwashed in the garage or the shed, or leave it on the kitchen floor for the little woman to clear away. This leads to very smelly nets and a certain amount of domestic friction.

Knock, knock.
Who's there?
Eileen.
Eileen who?
Eileen don your rod and bust it.

Fishing Through The Ages

A Green Dye for Horsehair Lines

Take a pottle of Allom-water, and put thereunto a great handful of Marigolds, let them boil well, till a yellow scum rise upon the water, then take half a pound of green Copperas, and as much Verdigrease, beaten to a fine powder, and put it with the hair into the water, and so let it boil again a pretty space, and then set it by to cool for half a day, then take out your hair, and lay it where it may dry, and you shall see it of a delicate green colour which indeed is the best water-green that may be.

Gervase Markham
Countrey Contentments (1613)

... And then explain to the wife why her non-stick pan is in such a state.

Who Runs the Club?

The Chairman

If 7-stone weaklings kick sand in your face on the beach, if your hobbies outside fishing are flower-pressing and embroidery, if you can't get served in the pub because the barman can't hear you, forget the chairman's job.

Authority is what you represent, and you'll have to exercise it at general meetings of fifty, sixty or more anglers, every one of them steamed up about something or other. As all it needs for an argument is two anglers, and all it needs for a riot is three, some simple multiplication should give an idea of the enormity of the chairman's task.

You need a high boredom threshold too, as your duties include chairing the various committees. It's bad enough sitting on one committee, but sitting on 'em all – not to mention the sub-committees – makes the Chinese water torture seem the thrill of a lifetime.

Still, there you are. You've got the job. Before you enter the room for a general meeting, make sure you've got everything. Pen, notepad, minutes of the last meeting, agenda for this one, gavel, shinpads, flak jacket, rubber truncheon and knuckleduster.

Establish your authority as soon as you walk in the room, before you've even got to the rostrum. If any members are slumping, scratching, sleeping or shouting, deal them a swift one with the rubber truncheon. If any in the front row are impeding your progress to the rostrum by stretching out their legs, stamp on their feet.

If any members are in possession of the Demon Drink, confiscate their hip flasks. Within a couple of minutes you should have enough of the hard stuff to see you nicely through the proceedings.

Your main duty is to ensure that the meeting is conducted in an orderly, democratic and parliamentary manner. All remarks should be addressed to the chair, and then only when the speaker has caught the chairman's eye.

Each speaker must preface his remark with the salutation, 'Mr Chairman' and not, 'Oi! Fartface!' or 'Just a minute, Four Eyes!' Respect must be maintained at all times, no matter how well the two know each other or how many pints the chairman owes the speaker.

A commanding presence and personal authority are the best means of keeping order. Weighing 18 stone, sporting tattooed knuckles and a broken nose are definite aids to a commanding presence and personal authority. Banging with the gavel does not always work, as the more irreverent of the members tend to break into 'The Anvil Chorus', 'Blacksmith Boogie' or 'If I Had a Hammer'.

Members should be aware that if the chairman stands up, the speaker must sit down. Should the speaker remain on his feet after the first public warning, he should be persuaded to sit down by firmer methods, such as having two stewards seek him out and clog him unmercifully.

The meeting can be brought to a temporary close, to allow tempers to cool, by the chair-

Smiling through . . . The chairman of Sludgethorpe Waltonians celebrates his thirty-third birthday in typical style.

man's walking out. This works well enough in other gatherings, but among anglers often allows tempers to rise, the chairman's absence being taken as licence to kick the living daylights out of each other.

A motion, after having gone through all the democratically approved amendments, and after allowing time for the bodies to be cleared away, can be turned into a resolution by a show of hands. Insist that the right hands only be raised, making due exception in the case of incautious pike or conger specialists, to discourage the less scrupulous members at the back from raising both hands. And have the stewards check that what appears to be a right hand is not just a cased rod with a glove stuck on the end. Total votes of 124 when only 63 members were present can cause some embarrassment when the minutes are read out at the next meeting.

If all this seems an unduly harsh summary of the conduct of angling club meetings, check with any former chairman of the club. You'll find him in the furthest recesses of the pub, pale and drawn, white-haired, toothless, twitching and gibbering over a triple Scotch. Sad to see him in such a condition. Especially as he's only thirty-three.

39

I Say, I Say, I Say . . .

The angler was out. Back home, his wife was in bed with his best friend.

The bedside phone rang, and the wife answered it.

'That was Fred,' she said to the best friend. 'He's out fishing with you.'

It's a Fact

Luring Them On

A British biologist has invented an electronic lure which can catch fish by tuning in to their brainwaves. The fish swim towards the lure, whose pulses lock their muscles rigid when they get close enough. They can then be netted at the angler's leisure.

The lure can be tuned to attract different kinds of fish. If you want pike, all you get is pike. Pike respond to twenty pulses a second, carp ten and eels five.

The biologist thinks that the lure may eventually replace the old-fashioned hook and bait, which would certainly please the anti-fishing lobby. But it may be too successful for its own good – using it he caught 169 pike in two and a half hours along a 2-mile stretch.

The Things They Said . . .

Don't Overdo It

> Overwork, n. A dangerous disorder affecting high public functionaries who want to go fishing.
>
> *Ambrose Bierce (1842–1914?)*
> *The Devil's Dictionary*

Nobody knows what happened to Ambrose Bierce. In 1913 he left America for Mexico and is thought to have had something nasty happen to him the following year in the civil war that was going on at the time. Either that or he went fishing and fell in.

Your Luck in the Stars

Taurus (*April 21–May 21*)

Slow, steady – and a bit of bull

Taurus is a methodical angler without being fussy like pain-in-the-bum Virgo. During hot spells you spend time studying the low water and noting holes and rocks on the river bed likely to attract fish. The evening before an outing you're down at the water, noting the conditions, checking on what natural food is coming the fishes' way, and pre-baiting a couple of swims.

Bait is seldom a problem: you have a natural talent for raising livestock which extends even to your home-reared maggots and the lobs in your wormarium.

Conservative and patient in your approach, you spend your time fishing two or three familiar stretches, rather than charging up and down the bank to try every likely swim. You have your own secret spots, too; slow moving and sturdy, you're able to barge through tangled undergrowth to reach swims that others would dismiss as not worth the hassle.

You make a good matchman, perhaps never coming out top, but always well up in the individual weights and contributing a regular and reliable poundage to the weekly team weight and your season's aggregate.

If you have a fault it's a love of singing, which is fine in its way but not always welcomed by other anglers when they're trying to concentrate. Full-throated renditions of 'Delilah' at seven o'clock in the morning, especially in conditions of severe hangover, are something they can do without.

If you have another fault, it's overdoing the food and drink. *Gourmet* and *bon viveur* is how you like to describe yourself. Glutton and tosspot is how others might put it, but at least you can hold your ale and don't make a fool of yourself in the pub like those who shall be nameless, such as Leo and Sagittarius. When it's time for the lads to get home to their nearest and dearest, it's seldom you who are in the wheelbarrow, though often you're pushing it.

The amount you put away may cause weight problems: you are the fattest sign in the zodiac. And although you carry your weight well, you have to remember to tread carefully on old and rotting jetties, and not to jump down from the landing stage into a thin-hulled boat. Those boats cost money.

Your cast-iron constitution means you have few problems with sea fishing, even in the roughest weather. While everybody else is turning green and consigning breakfast to the deep, you're happily munching a jumbo-sized beefburger, swigging a bottle of rum and giving out with some appropriate sea shanties. For none of which are the others inclined to thank you, though they're seldom in a fit enough state to complain.

You have a stubborn streak, which means that any latecomer to the bank who asks you to vacate his favourite swim is on a hiding to nothing. And a hiding is what he gets if he turns nasty about it; you don't suffer fools gladly and are usually big enough to make your point. (If he's a Scorpio, though, forget it. You fight clean; Scorpio fights dirty.)

You don't suffer bores gladly, either, and have a gentle method of cutting short the monologue about the one that got away. 'Boring old twit,' you say. 'Why don't you sit down and shut up?'

Normally fearless, frightened of nothing from banzai bailiffs to raging bulls, you do have a phobia about small things. Spiders or wasps can put you in a panic, and if anything creeps up your trouser leg on the bank, you're off your basket like a flash, screaming blue murder and trying to swat it before it can reach anywhere vital.

And talking about things in trousers, you're a bit of a ladies' man. Ruled by Venus, you are, which is as good an excuse as any. This has been known to cause the odd bit of ill-feeling among husbands at the club dinner and dance, and they have been known to express their disapproval by subtle hints such as breaking a chair over your head.

Too sensitive, some people.

It's Not a Fact

Fearsome Fish

Should you ever be fishing in the United States, especially around April 1, be on your guard against stories of mythical and monstrous fish. Known as 'Paul Bunyan' stories, after the tall tales of the legendary American lumberjack, they're told by local yarn-spinners to visiting greenhorns. These are some of the fish that Bunyan encountered during his days in the wilderness:

Cougar Fish
A huge and ferocious fish which infested the Big Onion river. Its forefins were tipped with long claws, with which it pulled lumberjacks off floating logs into the water, where it ate them. Paul Bunyan, who spent a lot of time on floating logs, offered a huge reward for every cougar fish caught. Unfortunately, he had a voice which carried for miles. The cougar fish heard him and thereafter were on their guard. To this day, not a single one has been taken. Him and his big mouth . . .

Giddy Fish
A sociable fish, swarming in shoals, and given to imitating the actions of one another. That, and the fact that their flesh was the consistency of rubber, made them very easy to catch through holes cut in the winter ice.

The trick was to scatter some dry groundbait into the ice hole. When the first giddy fish surfaced, it was hit on the head with a canoe paddle, causing it to bounce up and down. When the rest of the shoal saw this, they would start bouncing up and down as well. Before long, they'd all bounce themselves out of the water and on to the ice.

Goofang
It was 'about the size of a sunfish, only larger'. Which doesn't get us very far because the American freshwater sunfish is pretty small. What was special about this fish was that it swam backwards all the time. To keep the water out of its eyes.

Log Gar
A big fish, related to the pike, whose long jaws were crammed with great saw teeth that could cut right through a log in seconds. It wasn't so much the log they were interested in as the lumberjack on top. It can't have been much fun being a lumberjack.

Upland Trout
Apprentice lumberjacks and tenderfeet were sent out into the woods to catch these fish, which made delicious eating. They weren't easy to catch, though: they made their nests high in the trees, flew through the forest, but never went into the water. Casting among the trees made a hell of a mess of the terminal tackle.

Whirligig Fish
A relation of the giddy fish, though not nearly so bouncy, the whirligig fish always swam in circles – luckily for them, not ever-decreasing ones. Like the giddy fish, they were taken through holes in the ice. The trick here was to smear the edges of the holes with bacon fat. When the fish smelled the fat, they would swim round the edges of the holes, getting frantically faster and faster, until they whirled themselves out of the water altogether and on to the ice.

The Americans don't have a monopoly on peculiar fish, though. Britain has its own, especially in the industrial north, where two centuries of pollution has caused new species to develop. Among them are:

Toothless Pike (*Esox gummius*)
Early in its evolution, this fish took to hanging around the outfalls of black pudding factories and living off the nutritious waste products. Gradually it lost all its teeth through lack of use and developed a sucking action similar to that of toothless customers in tripe restaurants before the National Health Service.

Hacking Carp (*Cyprinus coffitup*)
Every time it breathes in it goes into a coughing fit, a result of grubbing around coal-washing plants and eating the cigarette ends thrown into the canal by generations of match anglers. Cigarette ends, especially those of high-tar non-filter tips, are a deadly bait. The carp's coughing fits give a curious action to the float, which dives straight under and then shoots back to the surface accompanied by a cloud of bubbles and gasps of, 'Ah'll give 'em up termorrer . . .'

Cloth-Eared Dace (*Leuciscus loppilugs*)
This is found around the outfalls of foundries and steelworks, where it has paid for the comfort of warm water by going stone deaf from the noise. An angler who asks his mate, 'What do you think they'll be going for today – maggies or bread?' is likely to be confronted by a cloth-eared dace sticking its head out of the water and asking, 'Yer what?'

Gormless Gudgeon (*Gobio goonio*)
A game little fighter, in fact positively aggressive as a result of its brain being affected by its chemical-saturated environment. Get one of those on your line and next minute it's up on the canal bank offering to take you on with one fin tied behind its back. After a stream of threats and abuse, which cannot be repeated here, its parting words are usually: 'And that goes for your bloody cat as well!'

Confucius he say,
Man with spinner up nose
Dink it dot berry fuddy.

Great Angling Discoveries

Refraction

Refraction is the principle of light which causes light rays to bend at the surface of the water, and which explains why a fish might see a standing angler and miss a seated one.

You can prove the principle with a simple experiment. Place a coin in a pudding basin and walk backwards until the rim of the basin hides the coin from your sight. Then get a friend to pour water slowly into the basin.

Before the basin is full, you will see the coin. Nothing has changed except for the water: you, the basin and the coin have not moved. The coin represents the fish, the edge of the basin the bank; the water represents the water and you represent you.

Messing about with pudding basins like this is not a very exciting thing to do, but it does help to pass the time.

The effect of refraction on an angler's vision after he's spent a morning squinting at 5 p pieces in pudding basins. The same effect can be brought about by too many whisky chasers at the club do.

I Say, I Say, I Say . . .

'This gaff's useless!'
  'What's wrong with it?'
  'Well, the head's fallen off twice and now the handle's come out.'

Angling's Big Questions

Why the Close Season?

One school of thought says that a coarse close season is unnecessary, that the fish would not be affected adversely if anglers were allowed to fish the whole year through. Another school holds that the three-month lay-off is essential. Certainly it does have some effects which are beneficial to both fish and fishers. Among these are:

1. It allows the fish to breed without distraction and to recover after so doing.
2. It allows the waterside wildlife to breed without distraction and to recover after so doing.
3. It allows the angler to breed without distraction and to recover after so doing.
4. It gives time for the bank to be cleared of litter and the waterside growth to recover from nine months' concentrated trampling.
5. It gives time for the angler's garden to be cleared of litter and the plants to be rescued from nine months' total neglect.
6. It allows anglers to re-establish contact with their loving wives, should they still be around, and to be introduced to their children. ('I'd like you to meet Daddy, darling. Now promise you'll be brave . . .')
7. It allows single anglers to make contact again with their girlfriends, should they still be around, and unattached ones to find a soulmate for a three-month burst of mad, passionate love.

8. It allows concentrated and objective study of the water, uninterrupted by the need to fish, to note promising runs, underwater topography or other special features which hitherto may have gone unnoticed.

9. It allows time to search for fresh pubs within reach of the water and unhurried sampling of the brews in each. Which is a bit more like.

10. It allows the bailiff time to walk the banks and check the state of them after nine months' continual wear and tear. And time for him to recover from the ensuing apoplectic fit.

11. It gives match stewards a break from their arduous task of keeping order and discipline, and allows them time to take whatever form of treatment their post-season condition demands (intensive care, Freudian analysis, psychotherapy) or to take courses in skills likely to be useful in their vocation (karate, kung-fu, clog-fighting, strangleholds and hairlocks, use of the rubber truncheon and arm-breaking in three simple movements).

12. It allows landlords of fishing pubs to get away from it all for a while to Tenerife or the Bahamas; to make good the season's wear and tear on their establishments; to trace the funny smells to long-dead pike lost behind radiators, and to add up how much the anglers have left owing on the slate.

13. It allows bank managers respite from demands for overdrafts for tackle and bait which is then either broken, lost, snagged, or simply chucked in the water. Bank managers do not understand this. Funny lot.

14. It allows the angler time to check over his tackle, clean and repair it, and replace any bits damaged beyond recognition. This he does in a frantic ten minutes late on June 15.

Knock, knock.
Who's there?
Tuna.
Tuna who?
Tuna piano. You'll get nowhere trying to tuna fish.

Knock, knock.
Who's there?
Harry.
Harry who?
Harry up – here comes the bailiff again.

Knock, knock.
Who's there?
Kipper.
Kipper who?
Kipper way from my swim.

It's a Fact

The Yanks Are Coming

In 1987 the Americans invaded Siberia – American anglers, that is, in pursuit of the legendary monster trout known as the Giant Taimen. The anglers have been allowed in under a unique agreement worked out in 1986 between Russian and American fishing and conservation groups.

The taimen, found nowhere else but the cold waters of Siberian rivers, certainly sounds worth fishing for: it can grow to more than 100 lb, and 40 lb fish are common.

The Angler's Guide to May

This is the month when you really feel that Spring is here and Summer's not far behind. The leaves are fresh on the trees and everywhere is smothered with blossom. Good-to-be-alive month, this is.

It's the month when the dyed-in-the-wool coarse angler should get himself sorted out, ready for next season. Mend or replace any worn or damaged tackle; check the catalogues for the latest additions; check that his fishing outfit is in good repair; that his wellies haven't perished or that mice aren't nesting in them. And renew his club membership. It's no use waiting until the second week in June, when club secretaries are working around the clock to send out membership certificates – and by which time the lists may have closed anyway.

For the game fisherman, May is a really magic month, with hatches getting more frequent and prolific.

Novice or cack-handed trout men can look forward to the period in late May or early June when the mayfly hatch is on the water and the fish are feeding as if there's no tomorrow. Duffers' Fortnight, it's known as. For a couple of weeks, so it's said, the veriest duffer cannot fail to catch fish.

In the main it's true, and the most gormless and ham-fisted can stock up with enough stories, suitably embroidered, to last him the rest of the season.

On some waters, however, Duffers' Fortnight can be affected by the application of Sod's Law, which decrees that the trout are scoffing some other insect which is hatching in quantity at the time and totally ignoring the mayfly. This has been known to lead to mass outbreaks of hysteria, alcohol poisoning, wife-beating and cat-kicking.

It's a Fact

Go to Work on a Worm

Earthworms are good for you – non-fattening and full of protein. They're plentiful, too, with fifty species in Britain alone, so it's surprising that they haven't caught on as a cheap and nourishing meal.

They have in the States. An American worm farm holds an annual earthworm cookery contest and gets entries of about 3,000 recipes.

The winning recipe of a cooking competition sponsored by the North American Bait Company was Earthworm Applesauce Surprise Cake. Anyone who ate it without knowing the ingredients would certainly be in for a surprise.

British marines on a television survival course in the wilds in 1985 had to live off the land, eating whatever they could trap or find. One gallant lad finished up eating earthworm omelettes.

The largest earthworm in the world is a South African species with a record length of 22 ft 6 in. A few of those would solve any angler's bait problem. As would the largest sea worm, the Bootlace Worm. One washed up in Scotland was 180 ft long. Difficult to get into the average tin.

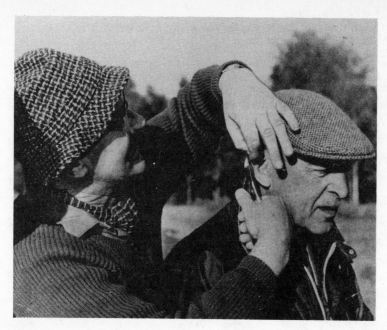

Traditional Angling Techniques

It can happen to the best of us. The late, great Dick Walker removes a nymph from the ear of Colonel Crow, famous Hampshire Avon salmon angler. With Dick's casting skill, it's unlikely that he was responsible for putting the hook in, but he certainly knew how to get 'em out.

Colonel Crow, as befits a military man, is keeping a stiff upper lip.

Know Your Tackle

The Rod Rest

A pointed stick of metal or alloy with a V- or U-shaped end, upon which the rod is rested after casting out to save the angler becoming fatigued and to allow him to light his fag, scratch his bum, pick his nose or wander off downstream to pester other anglers.

All but the sturdiest rod rests quickly become bent from being pushed too hard into dry or stony banks, jammed between the masonry lining the canal towpath, or used to open obstinate beer cans.

Another main cause of damage to rests is their use as weapons during bankside disputes which get so heated as to result in outbreaks of swordplay. Cyrano de Bergerac (1619–1655), in his day the finest swordsman in all France, is believed to have discovered his fencing skills during the Seine Junior Championships of 1629. With his rod rest he belaboured urchins from the rival team who tried to distract him by doing Schnozzle Durante imitations.

Rod rests are occasionally inserted up the nostril or other appropriate orifice of an angler caught cheating in a match. Less often they are sat upon by absent-minded anglers who have failed to note their position, which can damage the rests quite considerably. As the angler is also damaged quite considerably, he tends not to do it twice.

Traditional Angling Techniques

Tree fishing. An invaluable aid to research into the nesting habits of commoner British birds.

Fishing Through The Ages

Getting Their Goat

The ancient Romans believed that the spawning urge of a large fish in the Adriatic sent the males ashore in search of female goats. Local fishermen used to tether a goat on the beach and capture the fish as they charged ashore for a bit of how's-your-father.

More humane and less ancient Romans, presumably affected by the sight of the goats' watering eyes, put up straw dummies to achieve the same result.

Suggestions that this story is a load of old cobblers have been strenuously denied by historians and purveyors of goats around the Adriatic.

The Things They Said . . .

Stuff It And Be Damned

I am satiated with fishing stories – there's no truth in them! The man who caught that fish [stuffed in a glass case] is a blasted liar!
George Robey (1869–1954)
at a Piscatorial Society dinner

It's a Fact

Short Smelt Want

In January 1977 Peter Christian came first out of 107 competitors in a fishing match in Norfolk, with a catch so extraordinary that it made the record books. It was a smelt weighing $\frac{1}{16}$ oz, the smallest catch ever to win a competition. Rumour has it that it didn't put up much of a fight.

Who Runs the Club?

The Treasurer

The job of treasurer can sound attractive to the uninitiated or unprincipled. Collect the subs, pay the bills, oversee the bar accounts and social funds. Be plied with free pints by committee men who want a bit more cash for their own special projects, by tackle dealers offering gear at special discounts, and perhaps have the odd bit of loose change over for a further few jars.

Easy peasy. In which case, forget it. The post is not one for the amateur or the sticky-fingered. It's responsible, it's tedious, it's time-consuming, it's thankless and it's boring. It also demands a degree of accounting or book-keeping skill possessed usually only by professionals: accountants, bank managers, bookmakers, Gnomes of Zurich and the like.

Essential attributes of any treasurer are a pin-striped suit in sober colours, well-polished black shoes, a neat haircut and a miserable expression. A treasurer wearing a curly-brim trilby, multi-coloured kipper tie, camel-hair overcoat and two-tone co-respondent's shoes does not command the same respect. Know what I mean, John?

The miserable expression is especially important: any treasurer who looks less than funereal is immediately suspected of un-professional conduct, such as enjoying himself.

Among the first of the treasurer's many duties is collecting the annual subscriptions from members. This means, first of all, collecting them in real money; refusing post-dated cheques, foreign currency, IOUs, pawn tickets or ante-post betting slips.

You should give each member an official receipt, not just shove the cash in your pocket and bounce across to the pub whistling 'We're in the Money'.

In fact you should be careful of bouncing across to the pub at all, or indulging in any public behaviour which implies a state of financial well-being. Any display of affluence, such as a new car, new tackle, an extension to your wormarium, or even buying a drink, can result in ugly rumours starting to fly.

Collecting sounds a straightforward operation until you actually try it. The hard-luck stories would have the average gauleiter in tears: you couldn't really see members' kids without shoes, couldn't really be responsible for having the bailiffs in or mothers-in-law put down. The number of people awaiting a Girocheque, a pay cheque, a bonus, a horse to come up, a pools win or just for their ship to come in, is a social phenomenon you've never encountered before. And the number of members who dematerialise or are carried out in a dead faint as soon as you walk into a room makes you wonder whether your best friends should be telling you something.

You are given custody of the official cheque book, from which you make any payments due from the club. Sounds like a handy thing to have in moments of personal financial stress. And so it would be, if it weren't for the fact that each cheque needs two signatures; yours and another official's, usually the chairman's. This might seem like a slur on your character, an implication that people don't trust you. But it's the normal practice suggested by banks for the management of club affairs. Not that they don't trust *you*: they don't trust *anybody*.

Entries of transactions in the cash book should be made as soon as possible; you must be able to produce statements of accounts at all club meetings, not just at the end-of-year totting-up for the annual general meeting. It's no use standing there, pulling tattered receipts from your pockets or out of a biscuit tin.

You've got to keep track, too, of expenditure made by such officials as the match secretary, freshwater captain and sea commodore. All of whom invariably, at the last minute, stand there pulling tattered receipts from their pockets or out of a biscuit tin.

At the annual general meeting you have to recommend ways of keeping the club on an even financial keel, which usually means keeping expenditure down (not fishing so many matches; reducing the subsidy on bar prices) or increasing the subscriptions. Members are unanimous in their reaction to the proposals: they don't like either of 'em. They may express their disapproval by the time-honoured methods of a show of hands or throwing things.

The treasurer has many other duties which often go unrecognised as part of his workload: keeping track of the club's material assets such as tackle, trophies, badges and fishing waters. If the club's turnover is large enough, he also has to wrestle with the Customs and Excise over VAT.

At the end of the year, if he produces a set of messy and inaccurate accounts which give a false picture of the club's financial state, he is likely to be very unpopular. If he produces a set of immaculate accounts which give an exact picture of the club's financial state, he is likely to be more unpopular.

So you've a lot to consider before you stand for nomination as treasurer. Take advice. And the best advice of all is: let somebody else do it.

It's a Fact

On The Fiddle

Cheating in sea fishing matches in the United States is so rife that the Texas Bass Association now puts winners through a lie-detector test before handing over the winnings.

Big money is the cause of the cheating. When the Texas prizes – anything from $30,000 to $100,000 – replaced the original modest and tasteless trophies, catches soared astronomically. It wasn't just because more skilled anglers were tempted by the loot: naughty persons were getting into the act. One fish-running ring alone, for instance, was estimated to have won $250,000 illegally by smuggling out fish to competing anglers.

Not that it couldn't happen here; cheating happens everywhere. It's on a more modest scale in Britain, of course, but still common enough to worry angling bodies. British cheating techniques include:

STUFFING lead shot down the gullets of fish to increase the weight.

INSERTING a straw in a fish's vent and blowing to increase the size (not recommended if the fish is likely to be suffering from flatulence).

TAKING fish to the water stuffed down wellington boots or hung in plastic bags inside the jacket.

LOBBING toxic substances, such as soap or punctured shampoo sachets (preferably medicated) into an opponent's swim.

TAKING advantage of the jostling at a weigh-in to pass the same fish through the scale basket twice.

FISHING together as a syndicate with, say, five anglers fishing side by side in beach competitions. The centre man is to be the winner; the others slip him the fish they catch. They pretend not to know each other, and if the winner's catch is challenged, the other four offer themselves as independent witnesses.

STARTING to fish before the official time, and fishing outside the allotted stretch of water.

ARRANGING for the worse of two anglers to sit next to the top matchman. He then ruins the top matchman's chances by over-feeding the shared stretch with groundbait, making it possible for his more skilled mate to win the match.

Judges in a South of England trout match were suspicious when an angler weighed in two yellowish trout with small red spots. The fish in the river were silver grey with large red spots. It turned out that the angler had left his peg during the match, walked to a lake nearby, caught the two trout there and taken them back in his pocket.

A first-prize winner in a winter sea angling championship in Tynemouth won with three codling. It was discovered that the fish had been caught by somebody else the previous day, and that the angler had kept them fresh overnight by covering them with snow.

Such practices are, of course, highly reprehensible, thoroughly unsporting and positively un-British. Readers of this book certainly would not stoop so low as even to think of indulging in them.

If you *are* caught at it, don't tell anyone where you got the ideas.

Great Angling Inventions

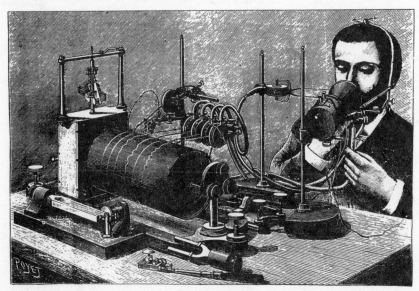

The Combined Lie-Detector and Breathalyser.

For use on anglers who have won a match, or lost it, by an incredible margin.

Your Luck in the Stars

II GEMINI

Gemini (*May 21–June 21*)

Keep talking – both of you

Out of the dozens of anglers lining the bank during a match, why is it always *you* who gets disqualified? It's not because you're up to anything dastardly; it's simply because you're Gemini. Which means you can't sit still and you won't shut up.

Even when you're sitting you're on the move: fidgeting, twitching, scratching, ear-tweaking and nose-picking. Actions innocent enough in themselves, but liable to misinterpretation by suspicious stewards, of which species there is no other kind.

When you're pleasure fishing, you're hardly ever on your basket. Most of the time you're wandering the bank, chatting up other anglers, admiring their catches or boasting about yours. Meantime, 100 yards upstream, the tip of your unattended rod is twitching madly.

Sedentary fishing isn't really for you: you're happier on the move with a spinning or fly rod. Even then you lack the patience to work a stretch over thoroughly and methodically before charging off to the next one. So either way – sitting down or standing up – you don't catch many fish.

Manually you're very skilled. You could save pounds by making your own floats and tying your own flies. So why don't you? Because you never finish them, that's why. Your boredom threshold is very low, and leaves you with hundreds of bits of unassembled floats and fluffless flies.

Another reason your catches never make the record books is that every week you're fishing with a different bait, giving the fish no chance to get used to one before you've switched to another.

Though you're naturally gregarious and fond of a natter, you really should go fishing alone. Apart from the fact that you're easily distracted, you don't like advice and you can't take criticism. The way you fish, there's plenty of both, especially from Leo and Scorpio. Bloody know-alls.

You're not above faking or botching to get the result you want, so that if ever you did finish stuffing that 3 ft pike, your friends would be amazed to find that it had grown posthumously to 4 ft.

They'd be impressed, too, with your story of how the pike fought like a tiger, how you played it for an hour with your rod bent double before finally getting it to the boat. They'd be less impressed with the truth: that you spotted it basking and brained it with a paddle.

Though your fishing tales are a bit over the top, you're quite popular in the pub for your ready wit and gift of the gab. So your stories are always in demand, even though your listeners run the risk of having their pints knocked over because of your habit of gesticulating wildly, especially when demonstrating the size of your catch.

You're not quite so popular in the club because of your unpunctuality – you're the one the coach always has to hang back for, always last at the weigh-in – and your tendency to gossip. You know everything about everybody and delight in spreading the news about who's doing what and to whom, and what happened behind the clubhouse on Ladies' Night.

Not that you've any room to talk. You're a bit of a devil with the women yourself – the original love-'em-and-leave-'em type – so whatever was happening behind the clubhouse had nothing on what you were up to. Not just that night, either: one of the reasons you took up angling was to indulge in the delights of night fishing. And we all know what they are.

Though you might not look all that robust,

you're quite a healthy specimen, with all your activity keeping you fit and slim. Your one weak spot is your lungs, as you'll probably realise when a fellow piscator, annoyed at the gossip you're spreading about him or the attentions you're paying his good lady wife, tries to prevent repetition by the time-honoured method of shaking hands with your windpipe.

Some Common Angling Phrases and Their Meanings

Angling, like every skilled and specialised activity, has a language all its own. What is said often does not translate literally, but has a cryptic inner meaning.

Here, for the tourist or non-fisherman, is a short guide to some of the commoner angling phrases:

It's a Whopper!
I have hooked a fish large enough to make my rod tip bend slightly.
I do not entirely believe the story you are telling me about the record-breaking fish you caught this morning.
Scum of the earth/Bunch of roughnecks/ Absolute incompetents
The opposition match team.
Finest flowering of British manhood/Ace anglers/First division material
Our match team.
A shade under six pounds
One pound, four ounces, three drams.
I appear to have mislaid it/Left it at home
I did not, in fact, buy a ticket for the water, in the hope that there would be no bailiff doing the rounds today.
The fish always stop biting at this time of day
The pubs are open.
The most superbly conditioned fish I have ever caught
It only had one fin missing.
Not the best day of the season
I have snagged and lost several terminal rigs, broken the rod tip, hooked myself twice, been chased by a bull, booked by the bailiff, slipped in a cowpat and fallen in the water. Fish? Er . . .
There's more to fishing than catching fish
I did not have a touch all day.
I go fishing for the pleasure of it, not the glory
I did not have a touch all day.
I would rather go for one specimen-sized fish than fifty tiddlers
I did not have a touch all day.
The finest day's fishing I've had all year
I caught three gudgeon and a one-eye bleak.
Concentration, that's the secret
This time I was looking when my float bobbed.
I fish fine and far off
My eyesight's so bad I can't see the float.
Pith off!
The bullock's pith, which I am using as bait, has become detached from the hook.
Go away! Yeth, you!

I Say, I Say, I Say . . .

Two identical twins always went fishing together. One twin always caught a netful; the other never caught a thing. They could use exactly the same tackle and bait, could stand fishing right next to each other, could swap over spots, but the result was always the same — one twin couldn't haul out the fish fast enough, while the other wouldn't even get a touch.

One night the unlucky twin decided to do something about it. He crept out of bed, put on his brother's clothes, borrowed all his tackle and went out at dawn to the spot where his brother had been so successful the previous day.

For a couple of hours he fished, with not a thing to show for it. Then he saw a huge carp cruising towards his bait.

'This is it,' he thought, and tensed up ready to strike. But his float didn't budge. Instead the carp surfaced slowly and poked its head out of the water.

'Morning,' it said. 'Where's your brother?'

Those Were The Days . . .

Fly rods at 10s 6d (52½ p), Scotch at 2 guineas (£2.10 p) a dozen bottles. Angling magazines at a penny and 2d per copy. Can't be bad.

The only snag is that if you'd been able to buy them at those prices you would no longer be in a fit state to enjoy them, i.e. you'd be dead.

1894, it was. Curse it.

It's a Fact

Silver Salmon

A Dublin hotelier paid £536 for the first salmon of the 1985 season caught on the River Liffey. The salmon weighed 12¾ lb – which made its price £42 a pound.

It's a Fact

Beat That

Prices for salmon beats in Scotland rocketed by more than 350 per cent between 1977 and 1985. Four beats on the River Conon, 10 miles from Inverness, were sold in January 1985 for an undisclosed sum believed to be more than £2,000,000. Prices on a time-sharing basis soared to as much as £15,000 a rod for a single week.

A beat on the River Cassley in West Scotland was sold for an estimated £500,000, making the 1¾-mile stretch worth £54 a foot – and that was only for a half-share. The average annual catch of 364 salmon made each fish worth £2,800.

Which brings us to the one about the well-britched angler at the end of the week complaining to his gillie: 'One fish, that's all I've had all week. Do you realise that that single fish cost me £2,800?'

'Och now, sir,' said the gillie. 'Aren't you the lucky man that ye didna catch the two?'

Knock, knock.
Who's there?
Eileen.
Eileen who?
Eileen Dover too far and fell in the water.

Knock, knock.
Who's there?
Esther.
Esther who?
Esther any fish in this river?

Knock, knock.
Who's there?
Luke.
Luke who?
Luke where you're going – you've just stepped in my groundbait.

Knock, knock.
Who's there?
Vaughan.
Vaughan who?
Vaughan day I might catch a fish on this river.

Confucius he say,
Dibbling your dropper
Need explaining to copper.

53

The Angler's Guide to June

The Glorious Sixteenth! Waheee!

It's not only anglers who welcome the first day of the coarse season. Their wives, too, are overjoyed.

At last the husbands are out from under their feet. The little women can turn over and get some sleep after nights broken by the sound of tackle being checked and assembled, dried crusts being ground and the blender going full blast downstairs as the secret groundbait ingredients are prepared. At last they can tidy up the house without having to step over piles of gear laid out in untouchable mounds.

Many anglers make an early start, getting to the water late on June 15 in an attempt to catch the first fish of the season. On the stroke of midnight the stillness is broken by the swish of thousands of rods, the whirr of thousands of reels and the splash of thousands of baits.

The first hookings of the season are made immediately. They are usually cows, sheep, trees, bridges, passing all-night buses, courting couples, other anglers, and gentlemen of the press incautious enough to attend the gatherings of such raving loonies.

. . . The tench has long been the symbol of the new season. There's a very special magic about the first tremble of the float on the mist-covered still water of a June morning. If it turns out to be a gudgeon, at least it's a start. The tench will be along in a minute.

The carp is another fish endowed with a strong Summer magic. Just as well, because if the dedicated carp men were sitting up all night and every night in the throes of a hard winter, they'd catch their deaths.

For the less skilful anglers, Summer is the time of gudgeon. Of bleak and dace, hard-fighting minnows and the occasional Tommy ruffe. So what? They're all fish. And after a few pints in a cool pub on a hot Summer lunchtime, every one of 'em fought like a tiger.

It's true what they say: there's more to fishing than catching fish. Ask any duffer . . .

Traditional Angling Techniques

An angler using the old-fashioned method of raking the bottom to attract gudgeon, and using the new-fashioned method of walking on water with the aid of polystyrene floats. He'll drown himself before the day's out.

Confucius he say,
Man with gozzer in pocket
Tickled pinkie all day.

It's a Date

June 1

Start of the coarse season in Yorkshire, beginning the 'stolen fortnight'. At the time of writing the Yorkshire Water Authority was planning to abolish the close season for still waters altogether. A stolen three months. That's more like it . . .

Father's Day

This is the second Sunday after Trinity, which means it generally falls about the time the coarse season opens: a handy time for fishing fathers to receive some appropriate presents.

Be nice to the kids for at least three weeks beforehand so that they won't think your changed attitude is merely in the hope of sordid gain.

Drop subtle hints such as, 'Oh dear. That reel of mine's not looking at all good. I'll have to treat myself before the season starts'; or 'Heck! The cat's been in my tackle box again! Chewed my best floats and tangled all the lines. It'll have to go . . .'

You could even try for the big one: 'My best match rod's got a set in the tip. I stand no chance of getting in the A Team now. And this year I'd really set my heart on it . . .' (The suspicion of a manly tear is not out of place as an accompaniment to a hint of this magnitude.)

All you have to do then is sit back and wait for whatever Father's Day brings.

It will bring, as it always does, a new tie, a set of handkerchiefs and a gadget for cleaning out your pipe.

You've got a rackful of ties, enough handkerchiefs to cope with a 'flu epidemic, and at least six gadgets for cleaning out your pipe. Just a float – one measly float – would have been welcome.

Still, at least you tried.

June 21

June 21 is the first day of Summer, and the year's longest day.

Anglers tempted to make the most of it, and fish on to the last remaining glimmer of light, should beware. By the time you've packed up the pubs will be shut.

Waaaah!

Fishing Through The Ages

Tickling a Tench

Poaching is as old as fishing, but it takes a brave man to own up to it. Certainly in Norman Britain, with the Conqueror's harsh game laws in force, it must have taken courage to confess:

> Sir, for God's sake do not take it ill of me if I tell the truth, how I went the other evening along the bank of this pond and looked at the fish which were playing in the water, so beautiful and so bright, and for the great desire I had for a tench I laid me down on the bank and just with my hands quite simply, and without any other device, I caught that tench and carried it off; and now I will tell thee the cause of my covetousness and my desire. My dear wife had lain abed a right full month, as my neighbours who are here know, and she could never eat or drink anything to her liking, and for the great desire she had to eat a tench I went to the bank of the pond to take just one tench; and that never other fish from the pond did I take.
>
> *The Court Baron* (1075)

That's the way.
Blame the wife . . .

Knock, knock.
Who's there?
Victor.
Victor who?
Victor his trousers on that barbed wire fence.

55

I Say, I Say, I Say . . .

The angler rang up the doctor and said, 'My little boy has just swallowed my porcupine-quill float. I'll bring him round in the morning.'

'In the morning?' said the doctor. 'But this could be serious, What are you going to do until then?'

'Oh, it's all right, doctor. I'll use one of my cane floats.'

Because of a 'flu epidemic, the angling club had to scrape together a scratch team for a very important match. The team really was more scrapings than scratchings, and the captain decided to give them a run-through on match techniques, right from the most obvious basics.

'Right, lads,' he said to the assembled team. 'Pay attention. This is a rod, this is a reel, this is the line, this is the hook –'

A voice from the back called out, 'Just a minute – not so fast . . .'

The Things They Said . . .

To The Manner Born

> As no man is born an artist, so no man is born an angler.
>
> *Izaak Walton (1593–1683)*
> *The Compleat Angler*

When he ran out of wise things to say, Old Izaak would chuck in something really banal. Such as you've just read . . . And then, a bit further on in *The Compleat Angler*, the silly old duffer came out with:

> Angling is somewhat like poetry, men are born to be so.

Which left everybody very confused.

Know Your Fish

Carp, Common (*Cyprinus carpio*)

According to the book:
Bronze or green in colour. A big, strong and intelligent fish of slow or still waters. Suspicious and moody feeder. Big carp feed mainly at night. Will take big baits of bread, worms, sausage, sweetcorn, boilies – including the traditional parboiled potato – and high protein concoctions.
Record: though bigger carp have been caught, the record remains with the late Dick Walker's 1952 fish of 44 lb (19.957 kg)
Between ourselves:
If you're looking for a sure way of going barmy or getting divorced, take up carp fishing. Not only is the larder stripped for baits every weekend, the little woman finds it hard to understand why you have to be out all night for three nights running. The hours spent in nerve-racking darkness, waiting for bites that never come, provide a steady supply of gibbering wrecks for the funny farms.

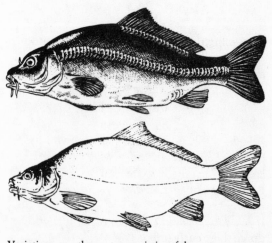

Variations on a theme; two varieties of the common carp.

Carp, Crucian (*Carassius carassius*)

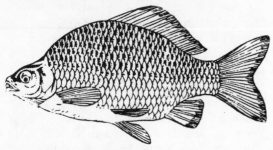

According to the book:
Looks more like a fat bronze bream than a carp. Habitats similar to the common carp. Baits should be smaller. Stockily built and a strong fighting fish for its size.
Record: 5 lb 10 oz 8 dms (2.565 kg)
Between ourselves:
Often a disappointment to the dedicated carp angler, who gets very peeved when he reels in a 2 lb crucian after sitting up all night in the hope of a 50 lb common carp. Other anglers who catch it by accident are quite pleased, really.

Tench (*Tinca tinca*)

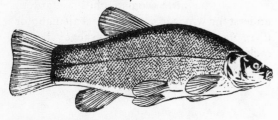

According to the book:
Strong, handsome bottom-feeder in still or slow-moving water. Fiddles a lot with the float, but makes up for it by its powerful fight. Careful weed clearing and pre-baiting of swims encourage tench to return to one spot. Wide range of baits: maggots, worms, crust or flake. Wheat, peas, sweetcorn, cheese and small boilies. Wild baits include wasp grubs, earwigs, caddis grubs, slugs, snails and swan mussels.
Record: 12 lb 8 oz 11 dms (5.689 kg)
Between ourselves:
If you're pre-baiting a swim, make sure you get down there early unless you weigh 18 stone and sport a broken nose and tattooed knuckles.

Word about pre-baited swims gets around, and there are some very early risers in tench-fishing circles. Don't wear your best clobber; a tench's slime ranks with that of bream and eel for quantity and quality, and starts to pong in no time at all.

Country Cures

Tench: The Magic Fish

The commonest superstition about the tench lies in its nickname of 'Doctor Fish'. Because its slime contains healing oils, runs the belief, other fish rub themselves against it when they are sick. And the pike, out of respect, will not eat the tench.

The pike appears not to have heard the legend: tench are part of its regular diet.

The tench's magic properties were once thought to cure humans. In the seventeenth century a common remedy for fevers was to apply a split tench to the soles of the feet.

It was also believed to cure yellow jaundice. Tench were split in two, placed on the soles of the patient's feet and around his heart. They had to be left in place for twelve hours, after which they were buried and replaced by fresh tench. ('After an hour they stinke,' cackled old chronicler John Aubrey.) Five such applications were reckoned to cure jaundice. The backbones were taken out of the fish beforehand 'because it will be uneasy on the patient' – presumably with a bony tench strapped to his feet he'd be tickled to death.

It's a Fact

A Lot Of Them About

How many maggots in a pint? Answer: 2,982.

A British angling journalist found out the hard way when he was given the job of counting a level pint of maggots for *Angling Times*.

One . . . two . . .

Your Luck in the Stars

Cancer (*June 22–July 23*)

Ah, you remember it well . . .

It's hard to know where to start with you. You're fond of water, which makes you ideal angler material. But your skin is hypersensitive so you can't spend too much time in the open air, whether you're being peeled by the sun, soaked by the rain or wrinkled by the wind.

You are also naturally clumsy, which means you spend a lot of time falling in the water you're so fond of. And every time you try a championship-length cast, your terminal rig finishes up in the trees. It's a gift, that's all.

You worry a lot. More than Capricorn, if that's possible. Security is the key to your personality, and you don't find a lot of that in the current angling scene. So you fall back on nostalgia. You hanker after the good old days. When the river was full of barbel and people dug sackfuls of worms to use as ground-bait. When there was no pollution, no heavy pleasure-boat traffic. When men were men and fish were fish.

The good old days were well before your time, which makes it even worse. All you've got to rely on are the stories you hear from old Amos in the pub. The good old days were well before his time, too, but that doesn't stop him lying about them and cadging pints on the strength of it.

Angling's changing too fast for your liking. Every week you're expected to use new baits, new tackle. Every week there's a new float, a new technique. You can't take all this. You go down to the same old spot you've been fishing for thirty years. Using the split-cane and greenheart rod your grandad used. And the wooden star-back reel. Not to mention the goose-quill floats. You scour the butchers and supermarkets in vain, asking for bullock's pith. And, because of your lisp, get thrown out.

When fellow anglers laugh at your old-fashioned approach, you brood. You go back home to read again the magic words of *Mr Crabtree Goes Fishing* and sigh for the days when a fixed-spool reel, known then as thread-line, was thought daring and a little bit unfair. When hints were given about the use of sugar in the preparation of deadbaits, followed immediately by the warning that on no account should you use sugar, because it was still rationed. Those were the days.

Your nostalgia makes you a great hoarder. You've got drawers full of floats that will never float again. Flies on rusted hooks that no self-respecting fish could look at without bursting out laughing. In your shed are half a dozen landing nets, wide-meshed and heavily knotted, that would get you arrested if you ever tried to use them. The same goes for the keep-nets, which are also grossly under size and definitely illegal. But you can't bring yourself to throw them away. It's the same with the gaff. And the fork-ended pike gag. Shortly you'll be consigning all your lead shot to your private museum. Can't have the swans popping off like that, if what they say is true.

But who knows? One day all these things might come back. Meanwhile, you spend many a happy hour playing with them.

Apart from Mr Crabtree, your reading is confined to old fishing guides and catalogues which advertise such delights as the Wharfe-dale fly rod, complete with one fly top and one short top, in a partitioned bag. Three sizes – 9½, 10½ and 11 ft – cost only 10s 6d each. (Ten shillings and sixpence: what lovely, sensible money it was then.) For the 12 ft rod you had to shell out a whole 11s 6d. For another 10s 6d you could buy a pair of Silenz noiseless boots, guaranteed not to put down the fish and warranted to wear for two years without soling or heeling. There were gut taper cast lines, eight-plait pure silk lines and tanned flax lines. Queen's Blend Scotch was 42s per dozen bottles. After that, can you be blamed for seeking refuge in nostalgia? It was a long time ago, but who is to say those days will never return?

Your present fishing activities? A bit erratic, a bit disappointing, except at the full moon. Then you're full of confidence. You get to the water, knock hell out of the fish, and bounce into the pub with tales of a thousand daring deeds.

Next morning you have a king-sized hangover, start to worry again and come out in a rash. Just tell yourself it was worth it.

Know Your Tackle

Floats

Floats are used to support the terminal line and bait in the water, and to indicate to the angler when a fish is biting. That's the official function, anyway, but mainly they're used for playing with.

Every angler has a huge collection of floats, of which he regularly uses about three. But they're great comforters during the close season when he can while away the fishless hours by sorting out his collection and singing 'Memories are made of this . . .'

Recent years have seen a vast increase in the type of float, with names such as wagglers, zoomers and duckers adding to the confusion. A new type appears almost every week, sells in thousands, is used a couple of times then bunged with the others in the bottom of the tackle box while the angler goes back to his tried-and-trusted quill.

Floats are popular choices among angling magazines for 'FANTASTIC FREE GIFTS!!!' because they're small, easily stuck down to the front cover and 'INCREDIBLY CHEAP!!!', especially if the supplier has been using computerised stock control and the com-

puter has bunged an extra couple of noughts on the instructions to the production department.

Few of these free floats actually reach the subscriber in a usable condition. Those which are not purloined by the paper boy are mangled as he stuffs the magazine through the letter box, or chewed by the dog. Still, it's the thought that counts.

Almost every angler at some time has a go at making his own floats. These have the advantage of being cheaper than shop-bought ones, but the disadvantage of sinking at the first cast or needing half a pound of lead just to make them cock.

Anglers who make their own floats can be recognised by their pebble-lensed spectacles and heavily bandaged fingers. Should they also bear evidence of being struck repeatedly with a blunt instrument, it means that their nearest and dearest has discovered the state of the dining room table or found the cat stuck to the skirting board with instant adhesive.

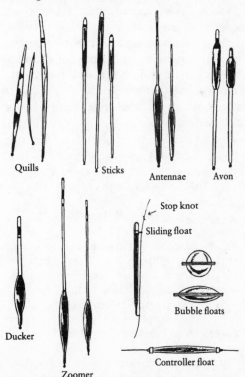

A selection of floats, just to show how complicated things can get. And these are only for starters.

Don't Forget to Write . . .

Living Off The Land

Fishing is an absorbing and time-consuming hobby, and indulgence in it can adversely affect other interests in the angler's life. A common result is the neglect of the angler's allotment and the consequent letter of complaint from the local council.

The last week of the coarse close season is the time you are likely to get the complaints. Early June sees a rapid increase in both vegetation and wildlife on the allotment. But not to worry: this is what you wanted anyway – plenty of wild bait. And just before the season starts is the ideal time to harvest the fruits of your labours.

The technique to adopt in response to the council's complaint is to have a quick hack around the allotment to chop down rampaging vegetation – not forgetting to collect the caterpillars and slugs as you go – and make it look as if some serious attempt at tidiness is being made. Then explain the reasons for the allotment being in the condition it was, assuring the secretary of the allotments committee that such a state of affairs will not happen again.

The Secretary,
Allotments Committee,
Sludgethorpe Town Council,
Town Hall,
Sludgethorpe.

Dear Sir,
Thank you for your letter of the 15th (your ref: NAF/54321/ORF) pointing out the condition of my allotment and advising me that failure to improve it would result in its re-allocation.

By the time you receive this letter, the vegetation on the plot will have been trimmed back to a level I am sure you will find acceptable.

If I may be permitted to explain the reasons for the other points mentioned in your letter:

1. *The buckets of decomposing fish guts.*
These were not just buckets of decomposing fish guts as such, but a home-made substitute for fish meal with which I intended to revitalise my vegetable patch. Any suggestion that they were intended to be used as rubby dubby or as groundbait for catfish I would have to regard as an uncalled-for and totally erroneous assumption.

2. *The maggots in the shed and the gnats in the water butt.*
I found that many of my neighbours on the allotment were being troubled by flies, especially bluebottles, and stung by gnats. To help eliminate the nuisance, I laid down plates of meat in the shed to attract the bluebottles, and filled up the water butt to attract the gnats.

This has, I agree, resulted in their breeding, but that is being taken care of. I have gathered up the bluebottle maggots, strained the bloodworms out of the water butt, and intend to dispose of them at the canal this weekend.

3. *The pigeon loft.*
I am aware that keeping livestock on the allotments is forbidden, but I thought it better to provide food and shelter for these particular pigeons, rather than have them rampaging all over the allotments to the detriment of my neighbours' crops. They have been kept in conditions of scrupulous cleanliness, their droppings being removed before the start of every weekend. Rather than pollute the allotment with these droppings, I have taken the trouble to mix them with my fishing groundbait and intend to throw them in the canal.

I am sure you will find these explanations satisfactory, but as an act of good faith I have removed the fish guts, plates of meat and pigeons from the allotment to the bedroom of my home, which also happens to be council property.

In case the housing manager should ask about the smell in the bedroom, as have some of the more inquisitive of my neighbours, you can assure him categorically: the pigeons don't mind a bit.
Yours faithfully,
Sidney Gungebucket
(Member Sludgethorp Waltonians A Team)

Who Runs the Club?

The Committee

Committees were invented so that club anglers wouldn't waste too much of their time fishing.

Committees pass resolutions, urge motions, propose, second and sometimes third. They move amendments to proposals and proposals for amendments to keep motions at a standstill. They speak through the chair and sometimes through the backs of their necks so that nobody can understand a word. If any progress is being made they raise points of order.

They organise the running of the club, so that the social evenings start as a shambles and finish in a brawl. They forget to order the beer for Christmas, which does nothing to restore members' confidence.

Pictured is an eighteenth-century committee wasting the club's valuable time by wittering on about something totally irrelevant. They obviously haven't realised that the bar closes in ten minutes.

Fishing Through The Ages

Right this way . . .

When a weir was built in 1778 at Acklington on the River Coquet, Northumberland, the locals put up a notice to direct incoming salmon to unobstructed waters nearby.

I Say, I Say, I Say . . .

'Did you catch much today?' asked the barman.

'A hundred or two,' said the trout fisherman.

'A hundred or two?' said the barman. 'Never in a million years. I'll bet you a fiver you didn't.'

'Done.'

'Right. There's the fiver. Where's your catch?'

The angler put a brace of trout on the bar and picked up the money.

'I told you I'd caught a hundred or two,' he said. 'And it definitely wasn't the hundred.'

It's a Fact

Charmed, I'm Sure

Worm charming is not cruel – and that's official. The RSPCA decided in 1984 that worm charming in charity competitions was not cruel, so long as the worms were returned to the ground after dark and not left lying there as a free meal for birds.

Worm charming? It's bringing earthworms to the surface by vibrating a garden fork, spade or stick in the ground, or by jumping up and down on the spot.

Thought everybody knew that . . .

The World Worm-Charming Championships are held every year in mid-June at Willaston County Primary School in Cheshire, with the entrance fees going to the school fund.

Each competitor operates in a 3 × 3 metre plot, and charms away for thirty minutes. Garden forks are used, with the optional addition of a smooth or notched piece of wood to strike or 'fiddle' the fork handle. Competitors squeamish about handling worms can appoint a second, known as a gillie, to pick them up.

Any form of music can be used to help the charming along, but drugs are definitely banned . . . though the rules do not specify whether for the worms or the charmer.

Charmed worms are released the same evening 'after the birds have gone to roost'. The presence of anglers among the competitors could mean that not as many worms go back as came out.

. . . No matter how charming you are, it *is* cruel to dig lugworms for sea bait. At least in some quarters.

In June 1985, three anglers appeared in court at Berwick-upon-Tweed, Northumberland, accused of 'taking, molesting, wilfully disturbing, injuring or killing a living creature, namely a lugworm'.

(The lugworm, *arenicola*, as every schoolboy knows – or bloody well should – is a highly-prized bait among sea anglers. The worms grow up to a foot long in burrows in the sand between high- and low-water marks.)

The case was referred to Alnwick Magistrates, 40 miles away, as the lugworms in question turned out to be dug outside the jurisdiction of the Berwick court.

But the law took its inexorable course. At Alnwick, in August 1985, the anglers were each fined the maximum of £20.

The issue involved, however, was not cruelty to the worms, but the fact that the digging of lugworms had been banned in parts of the nature reserve where the digging took place.

Four million worms had been removed in a four-month period, which left only one or two per square metre from an original population of thirty to forty. The anglers concerned were convicted of digging only six hundred and eighty-five worms, but seemingly it was enough.

And still the issue was not just the worms. The activities of bait-diggers at night, involving artificial lights, were disturbing the birds on the nature reserve, many of which fed on the worms. Not only did the birds have a lousy night's sleep, they emerged at dawn to discover their breakfasts had disappeared.

Traditional Angling Techniques

Two suggested forms of equipment and transport for the bait digger who goes about his business well away from the haunts of protected tweetie-birds.

Left is the equipment for the slow-and-steady method. All you need is a horse and cart and a well-muscled lady person, the traditional equipment for cockling in Morecambe Bay. The well-muscled lady person takes the strain out of the digging. The horse takes the strain out of carting the bait back home. You, meanwhile, have the traditional man's role of supervising. Somebody's got to organise things, dammit.

Above is the hi-speed method used by shrimpers in the Bristol Channel for getting the haul back quickly before the tide catches up with you. The sled takes the weight over the mud flats and you can get a fair bit of speed up by pushing like hell with your wellies. The tides are very high in the Bristol Channel, so any shrimper who doesn't push fast enough tends to go out of business. Known as the Enterprise Economy. Otherwise as Gurgle, Gurgle . . .

It's a Fact

Urban Griller

Keeping maggots in the fridge is a common enough practice, but anglers' wives had better hope that warming them up under the grill doesn't catch on.

A Mrs V. M. Hart of West Drayton, Middlesex, complained to the *Daily Telegraph* that sometimes, when the cold of the fridge had made them lethargic, her husband put the maggots under the grill to thaw them out a bit. Not only that, he was a bit careless when it came to rounding up the stragglers.

'Nothing annoys me more than finding stray maggots under the grill when I am about to do the toast for breakfast,' said Mrs Hart.

Bet there *were* things that annoyed her more, though – such as finding she couldn't do the toast anyway because her husband had nicked all the bread to stick in his groundbait.

Follow That Pong

The breeding of maggots for bait is big business in Britain, and British maggots have such a reputation for quality that they are exported by refrigerated lorry and jet plane all over Europe. Every week in Britain at least 25,000 gallons of maggots are produced.

So lucrative is the business that big breeders have to protect their farms with high wire fences, burglar alarms and guard dogs against attacks by the 'Maggot Mafia'. Gangs have raided farms and sprayed the maggots with insecticides, killing them by the million in attempts to create a maggot shortage. The gangs were believed to be acting for 'cowboy' breeders who found it difficult to sell their own inferior maggots.

Maggots are hijacked, too, by thieves who break in and cart them away by the truckload ... though usually it doesn't take long for the police to get on the scent.

I Say, I Say, I Say . . .

The squid was moping about on the sea bottom, feeling very poorly and sorry for itself, when along came a porpoise.

'What's up?' asked the porpoise.

'Oh, I do feel bad,' said the squid. 'Don't know what's wrong with me, but I'm so ill I'm sure I'm going to die.'

'Rubbish,' said the porpoise. 'A change of scene is all you need. Get on my back and I'll take you to the surface.'

The squid got on and the porpoise swam to the warmer, clearer water near the surface. Just then a huge shark came swimming towards them.

'Oi!' it shouted to the porpoise. 'I want you!'

'Can't stop!' yelled the porpoise, pulling the squid off its back and throwing it towards the shark. 'But if it's about money – here's the sick squid I owe you!'

The match angler was hauled up before the club secretary on a disciplinary charge.

'And what seems to be the trouble?' asked the secretary.

'The team captain called me a cackhanded, muddle-headed, incompetent halfwit!' fumed the angler.

'Is that all?' said the secretary. 'Aren't you perhaps taking this a little too seriously?'

'Too seriously?' stormed the angler. 'How would you like to be called a cackhanded, incompetent, muddle-headed halfwit?'

'I'd take it merely as something said in temper.'

'But supposing you weren't one?'

Knock, knock.
Who's there?
Athena.
Athena who?
Athena bailiff behind that tree.

64

The Angler's Guide to July

By this month the river is softer, gentler, and with a more even flow. This means that the fish are spread out more, are less inclined to stick with their traditional haunts. Weed growth is plentiful, and usually where there's weed there are fish.

Barring heatwaves, July is a good month. Pleasant weather, everything in leaf or bloom, plenty of wild creatures dropping off overhanging vegetation to the chub waiting below, and plenty of fish on the move.

The fly fisherman is happy. If he's not, he should be. All he has to do is count the flies that are buzzing around his head. If he can't match one of those, he's not really trying.

More of that later. Meanwhile, the bream are coming into their own, recovering from spawning and feeding heartily. The bream's habit of moving in shoals of roughly the same-sized fish, and of patrolling to a regular time-table, means that the dedicated and observant angler can whop in a whole shoal, especially if he's prepared to stay up all night.

It's the time of the photographs in the press of dozens of bream laid out on the grass, or packed into swollen keepnets, in front of an angler who is failing totally in his attempts to look modest. It's also the time of the letters of complaint from fish lovers – anglers and non-anglers alike – about such exhibitionism.

It's the time – and here we get back to the flies – of bites from creatures other than fish. The angler who prefers not to be eaten alive by gnats and midges, stabbed through and through by wasps, or chewed up by horseflies, is wise to wear a hat and to use some form of insect repellant. The little perishers always find somewhere to sink their gnashers, but it's worth trying to restrict their choice.

Here follows a list of old country remedies. For God's sake, don't use any of 'em.

One is a mixture of beeswax and turpentine dabbed behind the ears. Perhaps you don't get bitten behind the ears, but you do everywhere else. Another is a mixture of sulphuric acid and seal oil, which is supposed to ward off colds and rheumatism as well as keeping the insects at bay. It has the distinct disadvantage of leaving the user smelling like an old fish dock, which not only gets him thrown out of the pub, but pounced on by every cat within sniffing distance.

The North American Indians covered themselves with rancid bear fat. Very effective, apparently, but not highly recommended if you're using public transport.

There's always the good old good one: the smudge fire. This you build on the bank to windward out of damp straw, leaves, wet wood, old socks; anything guaranteed to raise a lot of smoke. Then you sit with your head in the cloud. Coughing.

Though the smoke does keep the insects away, it certainly doesn't have the same effect on the bailiff, who turns up and books you for lighting fires on the bank.

Traditional Angling Techniques

Fishing too close. Not so bad if it's your mate you're crowding, even though it could mean the end of a beautiful friendship. But if it's a 17-stone complete stranger with an anti-social disposition, it could mean a whole new set of teeth.

It's a Date

July 15

Legend has it that if it rains on July 15, St Swithin's Day, it will rain for forty days and forty nights. Scientific records show this not to be true.

Every angler knows that the only sure guarantee of at least fourteen days' continuous rain is to take a couple of weeks off for a fishing holiday.

Knock, knock.
Who's there?
Honda.
Honda who?
Honda the bridge, that's where the fish'll be.

Know Your Fish

Bream, Common or Bronze (*Abramis brama*)

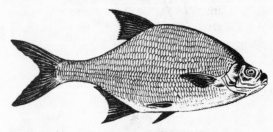

According to the book:
Shy shoal fish of slow or still waters, with regular cruising habits. Deep bodied, flattened from side to side. Very slimy. Takes stationary baits on leger or float tackle. Baits include cheese, bread, worms, maggots, casters, sausage, sweetcorn, freshwater mussel. Needs lots of groundbait. Big bream feed best at night or early morning. Fight described as 'slow but determined'.
Record: 13 lb 12 oz (6.236 kg)
Between ourselves:
Unless you're into a shoal of biggies, not the most exciting fish to go for. Fights like a wet lettuce unless it can turn broadside on to a current. Looks impressive from the side, almost invisible from the front. Covers you in slime, for which you're asked to leave the pub and are in trouble when you get home.

Bream, Silver (*Blicca bjoerkna*)

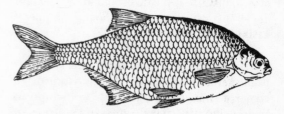

According to the book:
Smaller, silver-coloured relative of the common bream, with similar habits and the same shape. Largish silver bream are often mistaken for young bronze bream.

Record is open, with a qualifying weight of 1 lb (454 gms)

Between ourselves:
Even less of a fighter than the bronze bream, which doesn't say a lot. Can be told apart by a scale count and the fact that its eyes are bigger and nearer its nose. By the time you've gone through that lot, you've generally lost interest.

Gudgeon (*Gobio gobio*)

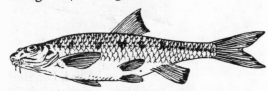

According to the book:
Tiny but game little fighter, fished for with maggots or small red worms on light tackle. Bottom-feeding shoal fish, feeds on hot days when nothing else is biting. Once caught in the hundreds on the Thames and cooked at *al fresco* Victorian fry-ups.
Record: 4 oz 4 dms (120 gms)

Between ourselves:
Looks like a dwarf barbel with measles. If it grew as big as a barbel it would outfight anything in the water. Often the butt of jokes in the pub, but it's saved many an angler from having nothing to report. Best not to put it in the keepnet with perch; not if you want to count the gudgeon afterwards.

It's a Fact

Fish Out Of Water

Carp have long been famed for the amount of time they can spend out of water. In the old days of monastery stewponds, carp were wrapped in wet sacks for the slow journey by horse-drawn cart to the town, and arrived at their destination alive and kicking.

In 1985, the greenkeeper at Yeovil Golf Club, Dorset, found a live 15 in long, 7 lb carp lying in the middle of the seventeenth hole – 60 ft away from the river. The day before, the River Yeo had burst its banks and flooded the course. The waters receded during the night, leaving the carp behind. It was soon found a new home – in the garden pond of the club chairman.

A carp now living happily in London had much further to travel. It came all the way from Israel in 1978, packed in ice, and woke up on a fishmonger's slab. The fishmonger gave it the kiss of life (honest!) and took it home that evening for his pond.

A fish which is even less distressed by lack of liquid is the lungfish of Africa and Australia. It can live buried in dried-up river and lake beds for up to three years.

More than you can say for the average angler who, deprived of liquid for three hours, tends to get highly distressed.

. . . We owe the frozen food industry to the amazing survival powers of fish. American businessman Clarence Birdseye (1886–1956) perfected his technique of freezing food after studying fish which had been caught, frozen to −50°F for several months and then thawed out. The fish were still alive.

Sorry, Fred . . .

A fish living off the Philippines can change sex at will. *Anthias squamipinnis* lives in small shoals with the females outnumbering the males by six to one. If a male fish dies or disappears, a female fish changes sex as a replacement. If a number of males are removed at the same time, exactly the same number of females change sex – and they never get their sums wrong.

Knock, knock.
Who's there?
Adeline.
Adeline who?
Adeline in this tackle box a minute ago – somebody's nicked it.

Know Your Tackle

The Basket

The fishing basket is used for carrying the beer and butties down to the water. With the larger baskets there is sometimes room for odd bits of tackle as well.

A disadvantage of the larger baskets is that when they're full the angler often has difficulty in standing up. Even should he manage it, he is prone after a while to Tiddler-Snatcher's Tilt, a condition in which one shoulder stays permanently 6 in lower than the other. Initially this merely gives the angler a funny walk and causes him to be laughed at by insensitive urchins. But in severe cases it can cause a fully laden angler to walk in a series of tight circles, a grave disadvantage when you're trying to reach the pub, and liable to attract the attention of the local constabulary.

Baskets are of several kinds:

The wicker basket has the advantage of keeping the angler's nether regions properly ventilated when sat on, so reducing the risk of Spotty Botty or galloping piles. It is the cause, however, of the almost equally dreaded Basket Bum, a condition in which the woven texture of the basket is transferred to the angler's hindquarters in a deeply indented reverse image. Basket Bum fades of its own accord within twenty-four hours, but those wishing to be rid of it sooner can try standing with their back to the fire for a couple of hours or ironing the afflicted area through a sheet of brown paper.

The wicker basket has the further disadvantage of being in demand by other members of the family. The kids borrow it as a prop for the school play or use it as a picnic hamper. The good lady wife uses it as a means of conveying the cat to the vet's. Either is OK so long as the kids remember to bring it back and the cat behaves itself. They seldom do.

Plywood baskets are fine, but carry the risk of splinters if ever they collapse, a not uncommon occurrence with well-upholstered anglers.

The steel-framed canvas basket is light and roomy, but can cause some very uncomfortable sensations, not to say risk of dismemberment, to any angler who sits down heavily on the edges of the frame.

Solid steel baskets are roomy and very strong, but inadvisable for winter fishing without some form of insulation or padding on the top of the lid. A frostbitten bum is not funny, except to other anglers.

The game fisherman's creel is light and easy to carry. It is also very upmarket, and can get you addressed as 'Sir' by status conscious barmen and bus conductors. But it doesn't hold much and is strictly for the wandering trout man. You look a bit of a wally carrying a creel along the canal, and may come in for some barracking or cries of 'Hello, sailor!' from the rougher element among the bleak-bashers.

I Say, I Say, I Say . . .

The angler came home after a day on the canal and found his wife sobbing hysterically.

'It was horrible!' she wailed. 'A man came here looking for you, found me here alone and made a pass at me. I tried to fight him off, but it was useless.'

'I'll kill him!' raged the angler. 'Tear him limb from limb! Just tell me who it was!'

'The captain of your match team.'

'Oh. Did he say whether I'd got a place on Saturday?'

The anglers had arrived to fish a match in a safari park. Just inside the gates of the park stood an evil-looking character with a pugnacious jaw, low brow, huge hairy hands and enormous muscles.

'Excuse me, steward,' said one of the anglers. 'Can you tell us how we get to the water?'

'No good asking me, mate,' said the apparition. 'And what do you mean — "steward"? I'm a bald-headed gorilla.'

Great Angling Inventions

The Combined Stool and Botty Protector

For lady anglers who find it difficult to carry a whole load of gear all the way to the water. Also serves to prevent undignified back-somersaults into cowpats.

The Things They Said . . .

Who's a Worm?

> Fly fishing may be a very pleasant amusement; but angling or float fishing I can only compare to a stick and a string with a worm at one end and a fool at the other.
> *Attributed to Samuel Johnson (1709–1784)*

Samuel Johnson was very clever, but he was grumpy, fat and smelly, with egg all down his waistcoat and given to belching and farting in company. He also knew damn all about fishing. So much for Samuel Johnson.

There is a theory, however, that he never said it. In which case you can ignore the foregoing rude remarks. He wasn't a bad lad really. Underneath it all.

Who Runs the Club?

The Fish Recorder

This is a nice little number, though not without its drawbacks. The duty of a fish recorder is to register every exceptional fish caught by members of the club. Which means that in most clubs he'll have a very quiet term of office.

He does not have to witness the fish; just to record it. Every claim must already have been verified by two independent, impartial and un-bribed witnesses. They will attest to the species, weight, method of capture, place and date.

But it is incumbent on the fish recorder to investigate any claim which seems the slightest bit suspect, such as a 3 ft pike which according to its alleged weight should be 4 ft 6 in.

The longer-term function of the fish recorder is to keep records which will be used for the Best Fish awards at the annual prize-giving; to build up a record over the years of the prowess of the club's specimen-hunters – and to make sure that a reasonably-sized fish does not become a bar-room legend and finish up as Moby Dick.

He should not object to his routine being disturbed, and should have an understanding wife. He may often be knocked up at three in the morning by a swaying angler who insists that his catch be recorded straightaway. His ever loving may come downstairs, disturbed by the racket, to find the pair of them trying to pin down a 25 lb pike which is flopping all over the new living room carpet and attempting to savage the cat.

Otherwise, it's a quiet enough job. Except when the recorder has to point out gently but firmly that the latest 'record' roach is really a roach/bream hybrid. Point it out to its captor, Big John. The large gentleman at the end of the bar cracking coconuts with one hand and throttling the match secretary with the other.

A general meeting of the club can then vote for a temporary fish recorder to officiate until the end of the season. Or at least until the plaster is taken off.

Your Luck in the Stars

Leo (*July 24–August 23*)

He's in charge

See that bloke who's just leapt from the boat as it approaches the landing stage? The one the skipper's fishing out of the water with a boat hook and a few choice words? Almost certainly Leo, show-off extraordinary, born to lead and to sup more than is good for him.

But you can't keep a good drunk down, and he's soon wrung himself out and got back to his usual role of organising everybody. 'Right – get fell in! Three ranks! All got your fish? Good. To the boozer ... By the front ... Qui-ick ... MARCH!'

Inside the pub he's first at the bar and buying drinks all round. The price his fellow members pay for this is listening to highly exaggerated accounts of his day's fishing, but it's usually worth it. Fibber he may be, but boring he's not; he's an accomplished storyteller and a frustrated song-and-dance man. When the saga is finished, he'll like as not leap on a table to belt out some good old good ones.

He has a great gift for working up enthusiasm in others. If there's a cold, dirty and boring job to be done, such as cleaning up a stretch of canal, Leo's the one to put in charge. He makes every man in the team feel as if the success of the job depends solely upon him. Soon they're at it hell for leather, cutting down weeds, dredging silted-up stretches and clearing out all the old prams and bicycle frames. Leo, meanwhile, clears off to the pub for a few

swift ones before nipping back for another burst of cheerleading.

For all his exaggerated stories, he's usually a pretty good angler. He loves the limelight. So he makes sure he catches something spectacular enough to ensure himself a place among the end-of-season prizewinners.

Whether or not he is among the prizewinners, his name will certainly get a mention. He donates a couple of trophies – the *Harry Flash Pursuit of Excellence Award*, the *Harry Flash Gudgeon of the Year Trophy* – which ensure that the noble name of Harry Flash is preserved for posterity and will appear annually in the club records and the local newspapers.

Leo is a great one for giving advice, whether he knows what he's talking about or not (it's the thought that counts, dammit), and is often carried from the water in a comatose condition after bending the ear of:

(a) a match angler who is disqualified for talking, with the clincher three feet from the bank, or

(b) a specimen hunter with a potential record fish practically beaten, but which breaks away as the angler turns round to ask, 'Yer what?'

His comatose condition, in case you've not already guessed, is caused by the fact that the angler has not reacted kindly to the interruption and has laid Leo low with a sackful of damp groundbait or the application of the right welly to the naughty bits. Not much of a choice, really, if you're on the receiving end, though the sackful of damp groundbait is reported to be marginally less traumatic.

Leo is always exploring new swims and experimenting with new baits. Not in the frenetic way of Gemini, nor the cool and scientific way of Aquarius. He's doing it because he's a leader, a pioneer, an innovator and an egomaniac. He wants to be first. First with the best. Not only does this ensure the adulation of the club members, and possibly a mention in the angling press; it means that he's got another stack of stories to peddle round the pub.

Club secretaries are happy to let him organise social nights. They know there'll be plenty of food and drink laid on – even if he has to donate a couple of barrels himself – and they won't be short of a cabaret. With a few pints down him, Leo will recite the whole of *Eskimo Nell*, render a few *fortissimo* Al Jolson numbers, and at the end of the jollifications lead the members in a conga file out into the night.

He will fall into the canal in an effort to cross the lock gates in the dark and spend the next week in bed with galloping pneumonia. But that's showbiz. A small price to pay.

Leo, you're lovely. In small doses.

It's a Fact

The Bigger They Are . . .

The world rod-caught freshwater record is held by a 360 lb sturgeon taken from Snake River, Idaho, in 1956. An even bigger sturgeon – 394 lb – was taken from the same river two years earlier, though for some reason wasn't granted record status.

Another fish which never made it officially was the biggest ever landed on rod and line in Britain: the 388 lb sturgeon caught on 28 July 1933[1] by Alec Allen on the River Towy at Nantgaredig, near Carmarthen, South Wales.

Allen was fishing for salmon when he hooked the monster. So terrifying was its emergence at the surface that a bystander fled the scene yelling. After twenty minutes, Allen's friend Edwin Lewis[2] waded in and gaffed the fish. The sturgeon jerked, straightened the gaff, and threw Lewis on to the bank with a flick of its tail that almost broke his leg.

Finally the fish stranded itself in a low run where Allen was able to brain it with a rock. It was taken from the water in a farm cart – it was 9 ft 2 in long – before a large audience of locals.

[1] The date is taken from a contemporary cutting. *The Guinness Book of Records* gives it as July 25. Allen's obituary in 1972 gave it as July 9.
[2] The *Guinness Book of Records* says Allen was helped by David Price. Alderman Price, a great friend of Allen's who died in 1975, told the story in a newspaper interview and named Lewis as the man who gaffed the fish.

A sporting (note the light-weight rod) Brazilian specimen hunter with a fair-sized *Arapaima gigas*, wondering how he's going to get the damn thing home.

A telegram to Buckingham Palace, offering the sturgeon as the royal prerogative, brought a reply to the effect that the King was not in residence and therefore did not wish to know. So Allen sold the fish to a Swansea fishmonger for £2 10s (or £2.50 in decimal currency). Allen, who died in 1972, was a commercial traveller for a fishing tackle firm. Hopefully he was better at selling fishing tackle than selling sturgeon.

He was quoted later as looking on the sturgeon as 'a bit of a nuisance'. He was a dedicated salmon fisher and the sturgeon had interrupted his pursuit. Dedicated salmon fishers will know the feeling; others could be excused for thinking that Allen was a bit of a nutter.

Though Allen's fish was the biggest landed on rod and line in Britain, there's still a possibility of something bigger. In 1937 a sturgeon weighing 507½ lb and 9 ft long was netted on the River Severn. In 1976, one of 572 lb was netted in the Danube, which isn't all that far away. Thought to be between eighty and a hundred years old, it contained 97 lb of caviar.

Another monster freshwater fish is the Brazilian *Arapaima gigas*, which reaches a length of 15 ft and a weight of 400 lb. Despite its size, it is caught by the natives on rod and line, though sometimes they cheat and give it one with a bow and arrow.

July seems a good month for big fish, as witness the 516 lb, 6 ft long Nile perch, netted on Lake Victoria, Kenya, in July 1978. Not only did the fishermen have their work cut out landing the thing: it took sixteen of them an hour to get it on the roof of a bus to take it back to town – where all they got for it was £40 from fishery researchers.

Netted, of course, it did not qualify as a rod-caught record. But it was certainly the stuff that dreams are made of . . .

It's a Fact

Terrifying Tinkle

British anglers have been warned to keep away from the giant hogweed, a relative of the cow parsley, which has spread southwards from its natural habitat in Scotland and the North of England.

It grows mainly on river banks, and by July it is 15 ft tall. Its hairy stem exudes a sap which can cause painful burns on human skin which is exposed to sunlight. More serious cases can result in a recurring rash. The old-fashioned nettle rash has nothing on giant hogweed rash, so anglers answering a call of Nature are advised to look before they tinkle.

It's a Fact

Casting for Cash

In July 1986, two teenagers fished a lake at Groby, near Leicester, for 13 hours without catching a single fish. They were just about to give up when one of them hooked a plastic bag. Inside it was £12,000 in foreign banknotes.

Confucius he say,
Angler who win
Get filled up with gin;
Angler who lose
Buy his own booze.

The Angler's Guide to August

Ah, August . . . The finest flowering of the English Summer. The warm, drowsy days. The noble trees in their fullest leaf. The hum of the industrious bees. The still waters, curling their mists in the early morning as the golden sun strikes the limpid surface. What could mar such idyllic scenes?

Kids!

That's what. Flaming kids. On the long holiday from school. Roaming the banks in droves, slinging in 4 oz leads from broomstick rods right next to your float. Getting bored after a while and skimming stones across the water. Or switching on their ghetto blasters at full belt, right in your ear. Or charging up and down having sword fights and stampeding every fish for miles.

Kids! Ought to be banned. Better still, transported.

But stay. That is not the attitude the mature and skilled angler ought to have towards the younger generation. We were all young once. And we can pass on to these youngsters the skills we ourselves learned through the patience of older anglers.

So sit beside me, little lad, and I will show you the way you ought to go; teach you the skills my own father taught me. Teach you all the art and mystery of the craft of angling that is in my humble power to transmit.

That's it. Sit down, stay low, don't move. Get your groundbait out, at the proper texture, into that likely looking eddy by the rock. Cast out carefully, looking behind you before you do, for safety's sake. Now keep your eye on the float. See, it's twitching! Don't be hasty. Strike just as it dips under – You've got it!

Why, you snotty-nosed little swine! That's the monster I've been after for weeks! And you've got the flaming nerve to come down here and snatch the thing from under my nose at first cast! I'll murder you, you little . . .

Calm yourself. Who wants the fresh water in hot weather, anyway? Nothing but gudgeon and bleak, and not a lot of those. And not only kids to contend with. Everybody's out: a million old ladies walking a million leg-cocking dogs; a million old fellers with nothing else to do but ask if you've had any luck; a million pleasure boats, with a million weekend skippers looking right wallies in their yachting caps; a million more kids in kayaks doing the Duke of Edinburgh award bit and sploshing right through your line; all the ducks and all the swans in the world homing in for their holidaytime freebies.

You're best out of it. Out to the sea for some bracing air and bigger fish. Not from the pier, either: that's crowded with once-a-year cack-handers knocking off kiss-me-quick hats on the backswing; crowded again with kids who keep fiddling with your catch and unaccountably avoiding the conger which might deter them a little.

No, it's the open sea for you, lad. Out on the briny, as befits the scion of a seafaring nation. Book a boat guaranteed to have no kids on it. Get out there, beyond the 3-mile limit, to the famous wrecking mark in the wind-blown, choppy water.

Ah, this is the –

Bleargh!

Groo!

Perrr-UKE!

Aaaarrrrgggghhhh!

Wanna die . . .

Hey, skipper . . . How much longer are we supposed to be staying out here? What do you mean, until the moon comes up? It must have come up. Everything else has.

One thing about sea fishing. You soon know when you've had enough. And it makes you grateful for the idyllic scenes you left behind on *terra firma.*

Kids or no kids . . .

It's a Date

August 9

Izaak Walton's birthday

Izaak Walton, author of *The Compleat Angler* and father of British angling, was born in Stafford on 9 August 1593, which has since given anglers a cause for celebration in a month when otherwise there's not a lot doing.

It's best to celebrate in one of the many pubs named *The Izaak Walton* in the hope that they'll be dispensing free beer in honour of the occasion. If not, there's no harm in suggesting it.

Walton died on 15 December 1683, which gives dedicated anglers another excuse to get wellied, and gets Christmas off to an early start (see December).

He used to be addressed as Izaak Walton, Isaac Walton, Isaak Walton and Izaac Walton. It can't have worried him much because he didn't seem too sure himself. In his marriage lines he signed his name with a 'C', but signed his will with a 'K'. On his tombstone, not that he could do much about it, he was described as Isaac.

The Compleat Angler has the distinction of being one of the world's best-selling books. It has the other distinction of being hardly ever read all the way through. The old lad is a bit hard going, wittering on about all sorts of things which don't have a lot to do with fishing, and padding the book out with hey-nonny-nonny-type songs and poems.

His hero, Piscator, makes a habit of accosting complete strangers and dragging them into pubs – Izaak was the son of an alehouse keeper, which may have had something to do with it – for jolly debates on the merits of different country pursuits. Piscator had a thing about milkmaids, too, once getting not only a milkmaid but also her mother to join them and sing a song (presumably saying to his companion, the hunter Venator: 'I don't fancy yours').

In spite of all this, there's a lot of fascinating stuff when Walton does get down to fishing. So don't give up altogether, just grit your teeth and skip the rambling bits.

Walton, incidentally, married twice and had ten children, which makes you wonder how he found time to go fishing at all.

Izaak Walton

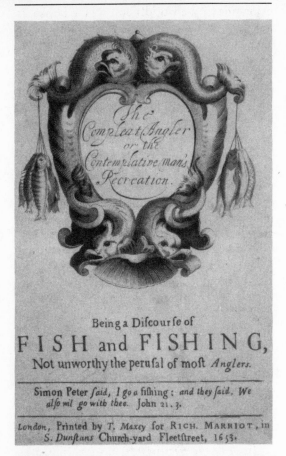

Title page of the first edition of *The Compleat Angler* (1653).

It's a Fact

Fish Blows Up Man

Sicilian fisherman Salvatore Monteverde, fishing off the coast of Catania in August 1985, dropped an explosive charge over the side to stun or kill the fish.

He was blown up and the boat was sunk when a fish seized the charge and carried it under the keel.

Salvatore had to swim 2 miles back to shore, and was not all that pleased about the incident. 'I'm sure the fish did it deliberately,' he said.

Know Your Fish

Eel (*Anguilla anguilla*)

According to the book:
Snake-like fish hatched in the mid-Atlantic Sargasso Sea. Journeys to our shores with the Gulf Stream as an elver and swims upriver. Grows to adult size then swims back to the Sargasso to spawn and die. Generally regarded as a fish of the summer and autumn; hibernates during winter. Best times to fish are the two hours before daylight and the two after dusk. Caught on lobworm, deadbait, liver or meat. Try to pump it to the top before it can wrap itself around a snag.
Record: 11 lb 2 oz (5.046 kg)
Between ourselves:
Eels are fine if you are fishing for them deliberately and prepared for them with steel trace, snap link, plenty of newspaper and a sack. Not to mention a mobile laundry unit. If you're unprepared or don't want 'em, they can be a flaming nuisance. Don't think too hard of the eel, though: just look at its face. The eel has the most delicate little face of any fish on the river, with a prim little mouth and small and beautiful eyes. Orrr . . . (End of soppy date bit.)

Knock, knock.
Who's there?
Nat.
Nat who?
Nat a fish all day:
how've you done?

Knock, knock.
Who's there?
Ivan.
Ivan who?
Ivan ibble on my line.

Know Your Tackle

Split Shot

Split shot are used to get the line out to the fish, to keep the bait on the bottom or at the required depth, and to cock the float so that it gives a better indication of a bite.

Split shot are shot which are split. Hands up anybody who didn't know. The split enables the shot to be clipped to the line. This should be done with pliers, as pinching them on with the teeth can lead to damage. The notice anglers take of this warning is evident by the number of toothless anglers about.

Most sizes of lead shot have been banned in Britain and replaced, hopefully, by an efficient non-toxic substitute. The banning is because of the number of swans suspected of having died from lead poisoning by swallowing the shot. Other factors, such as the swans' swallowing gallons of diesel fuel from pleasure boats every day, seem to have been discounted.

It's a Fact

What's Up, Doc?

In August 1978, President Jimmy Carter of the United States was attacked on a fishing trip by what White House aides described as a 'mad rabbit'.

He was fishing from a boat when the rabbit swam out from the bank – 'hissing and spitting' – and tried to climb aboard. Mr Carter picked up his paddle and brained it.

'It was a killer rabbit,' said an official. 'The President was swinging for his life.'

The rabbit was unable to comment, on account of being dead.

Who Runs the Club?

The Sea Commodore

The increasing popularity of sea fishing means that more inland clubs are making fairly regular trips to the coast for an outing on a hired boat. To make sure everything goes smoothly, it helps if the club appoints a sea commodore.

The very grandness of the title means there are plenty of applicants for the post. It's best to give it to someone with at least minimal knowledge of sea fishing or seafaring, and not just hand it to the first bloke with one leg, a crutch and a parrot on his shoulder who hops up declaiming, 'Aaarrrh . . . Jim lad!'

The appointment often goes to the commodore's head. The first thing he does is buy a jaunty yachting cap and burst out with phrases like: 'Ahoy there, me hearties! Luff yer mains'l and stun yer tops'l! Hard a-port by the starboard bow! And belay that friggin' in the riggin'!' Leaving the professional boatmen asking each other, 'What's that old twit raving on about?'

The commodore's initial duty is to make sure that sea bookings don't clash with freshwater outings. If the freshwater captain discovers that half his A Team is on the high seas when they should be fishing the needle match against their deadly rivals, he is not 100 per cent pleased.

His next duty is to make sure the bookings coincide with the tides. Sea fishing at a distant harbour means an early start. Giving the lads an hour's lie-in before leaving home isn't much consolation when the boat is discovered stranded high and dry with the next tide not due for ten hours.

The recommended way for the commodore to get to know any given sea-fishing venue is to visit the place, check the condition of the boats in the harbour, and then get to know the boatmen by visiting their local boozer and chatting them up. It is best if he makes a note of names and addresses before the serious drinking starts, so that next day he can ring them up and ask what was agreed before he was carried out.

Before boarding a boat it is advisable for members to hold a draw for positions. This saves all the unseemly shoving and pushing to be on first and grab the seats at the back, stops gangplank scuffles or kicking and gouging on the ladder, and generally ensures that there are no casualties before the anchor is weighed. (There's a good seafaring term: weighing the anchor. Sounds much more professional than pulling it up. Knowing it, when the skipper announces, 'Right. We'll weigh anchor,' stops you saying, 'No need to bother just for us. I reckon it's about a half-hundredweight.')

Once at sea, the commodore will note the general attitude of the skipper and the sea-worthiness of the boat. If the skipper just chugs out a couple of miles and drops anchor, instead of making for a proper mark, and then retires with a copy of *Playboy* and a mug of rum-laced tea – leaving the lads to their own devices – he's possibly not the most professional. If the boat capsizes, it's possibly not the most seaworthy.

The commodore should familiarise himself with the different kinds of sea fish, as many of them have dangerous spines or teeth whose danger the average freshwater angler does not appreciate.

'Careful,' he says to the angler unhooking a harmless-looking fish. 'That's a whiting, that is. Watch out for its teeth.'

'Teeth?' says the angler. 'What teeth?'

'These teeth,' says the commodore, jabbing his finger at the whiting's jaws. 'These – Aaaaarrrrrgh!'

During the trip he should make the rounds of the boat, checking that each angler is enjoying himself and not suffering too much discomfort from the unaccustomed motion. He discovers that most of the anglers are suffering enor-mously, and may attempt to relieve this by the administration of a time-honoured specific.

'Here,' he says, offering the angler a large tot of rum. 'Get it down. It'll do you good.'

Thirty seconds later, as the angler is draped groaning over the side, he comforts him with, 'That's right. Get it up. It'll do you good.'

At the end of the trip the commodore is responsible for the fair and orderly division of the catch. Before booking, he should have checked the small print and discovered whether the skipper was invoking the two-fish rule, i.e. whether the lads were allowed to take away only two fish each, leaving the rest of the catch for the skipper to flog at the local market.

If he has omitted to check, he may get some indication during the trip from the way the skipper is walking up and down, flailing at the anglers with a rope's end and shouting, 'Fish, yer buggers! Fish!'

Should the two-fish rule be invoked without warning, the commodore's duty is then to calm the lads down, dissuading them from stringing the skipper from the yardarm (or at least from the wireless mast) and from throwing his own dear self in the drink. As the skipper can point to the clause in the small print, he is usually spared. As the commodore failed to notice it, he isn't.

That's another quality essential for the full performance of the sea commodore's duties: he should be able to swim.

Country Cures

The Healing Eel

The old-timers didn't let much of the eel go to waste.

An old country method of avoiding cramp was to wear an eelskin garter next to the skin. It works for swimmers, too, it's said. So if you're expecting to fall in the water . . .

Sprains or swellings, which are easy to come by on the bank, used to be cured by the atten-tions of the Stamp Stainer, a sort of old-time physiotherapist. What he did was to jump up and down on the affected part. The cure was completed by binding the poorly bit with eelskin. Presumably, after the patient had stopped screaming.

Warts were cured by rubbing them with eel's blood. The eel's head was cut off and the bleeding bit rubbed on the warts. The eel's head was buried and, as it rotted, so the warts were supposed to fade.

The eel even cures a man of the Demon Drink. All you have to do, according to the old wives, is to put a live eel into his pint pot. Once he discovers it he signs the pledge on the spot. Probably in a state of shock.

How to Hold an Eel

The phrase 'slippery as an eel' was not coined for nothing, and the eel is the most difficult fish to unhook and return to the water undamaged. Holding it with a rough cloth is one answer, but it can strip the eel of much of its protective slime. So try this:

Slip the middle finger of the left hand over the back of its neck, and the two fingers on either side under its throat. Press down with the middle finger and there you have him; in a sort of three-fingered full Nelson. You've now got his head steady enough to take the hook out; the rest of him can wriggle away regardless.

It's a Fact

Pulling The Plug

Anglers who turned up to fish a stretch of the Chesterfield-Stockwith Canal, Nottinghamshire, one afternoon in August 1978 were mystified to find that the canal had disappeared – at least, all the water had for 1½ miles, and it was there when they'd knocked off for their lunchtime pint.

The mystery was solved when a gang of workmen returned from their lunch break. They'd been dredging the stretch that morning and hauled up a huge chain. What they didn't know was that on the other end of the chain was a giant wooden plug, two hundred years old and lost track of when World War Two

bombing in Leeds destroyed the records. They'd literally pulled the plug on the canal and all the water had drained away into the River Idle nearby.

ILL WIND DEPARTMENT: Though the engineers in charge of the job were a bit peeved at first, they finished up happy that the plug had been pulled. They'd been puzzled for years about a mysterious leak on that stretch of canal, and now they'd found the cause.

Great Angling Loonies

Speedy Sid Sillisod, from Solihull. In a hurry to get to the water. Not quite sure which swim to head for. And about to do himself a mischief.

Your Luck in the Stars

VIRGO

Virgo (*August 24–September 23*)

Boring old what?

You're probably the club secretary, being, as the sign implies, a bit of an old maid. A right fusspot.

You're ideal for the job, keeping records meticulously up to date, never forgetting to order the bingo tickets and match entry forms, keeping the trophies polished, insured and safely under lock and key. After a match you make sure the lads take their litter home and leave the bank as they would wish to find it.

A stickler for accuracy, you can put a dampener on tales in the pub.

'I landed this twelve-and-a-half-pound pike,' says Fred.

'Ten and three quarters,' you interrupt.

'On a two-pound line.'

'Five-pound.'

'And played it for an hour.'

'Ten minutes.'

'Who's telling this story?' asks Fred.

'You are.'

'Then why don't you bugger off?'

Not that you spend long in the pub. While the others are swilling ale, lying furiously, falling about and throwing up, you're toying with a half of shandy and mentally running through the subscriptions list. Old Sid over there: he's got the money to be guzzling double Scotches but he's twelve months in arrears. Must have a word.

And fishing? Oh, fishing. That's not really the bit you enjoy most. All those slimy worms and wriggling maggots. All that overripe cheese. A bit messy. Bit smelly. Can't stand mess and smells. And the fish themselves are so unpredictable. Can't stand unpredictability either.

But you go fishing because it's expected of you, part of the job. You certainly look keen: you've enough tackle to kit out the whole team, all of it in first-class condition. Even in the worst weather you stay warm and dry, protected by layers of waterproof clothing, windbreak, brolly, nose cosy, foot muff and hand warmer.

You worry about your health a lot; as well as dressing warmly for the bank, you carry a medicine chest with remedies for every ailment known to man and a few which haven't been discovered yet. The others, meanwhile, rely for a cure-all on the tried-and-trusted Scotch. Peasants.

But you do need the medicine chest. Apart from being a fully paid-up hypochondriac, you have a tendency towards rheumatism and backache, both easily contracted on a damp river bank. Better to be safe than sorry, you always say. Prevention is better than cure, you always say. You seldom say anything original.

You seldom do anything original, either. You fish by the book, using a conventional rod and terminal rig, conventional baits and conventional methods. You catch conventional fish, nothing spectacular, play them in textbook style and get them to the bank with as little theatricality or delay as possible.

You get home not too late in the evening, perfectly sober and looking as neat and tidy as when you left. Instead of slinging all your tackle in a heap on the shed floor, or leaving it on the hearth rug for the wife to put away – the angler's usual method of storage – you go through a strange ritual.

You take out the rods, wipe off any mud and sand, replace them in their bags and lay them on a special shelf. You dismantle the reels, clean and oil them. You wash out landing nets and keepnets, repair any holes, and hang them out on the washing line to dry. You check through floats, lines and hooks and discard any which are damaged, frayed or rusted. You dispose of surplus maggots and groundbait, and scald out the cans.

You then write up all the day's results neatly in the match record book and make extra copies for the local papers. Can't trust the press officer.

There may be time for a bit of float-making and fly-tying. You enjoy this and, unlike some we could mention, you actually finish making them. They work, too: the floats don't sink at first cast and the flies don't frighten the life out of the fish. Most unusual for home-made tackle.

After all that, it's time for your Horlicks and a good night's sleep. Early to bed, early to rise, you always say.

Boring old fart? What do you mean?

Did anybody *say* you were a boring old fart?

The Things They Said

The Hairy Eel

The origin of freshwater eels – we now know their spawning grounds to be the mid-Atlantic Sargasso Sea – was a puzzle to the ancients. As late as 1864 it was commonly supposed that if horse hairs were left in the water they would turn into eels.

Izaak Walton quoted several theories: 'Bred as some worms, and some kind of bees and wasps are, either of dew or out of the corruption of the earth'; 'Eels, growing old, breed other eels out of the corruption of their old age'. Finally he affirmed: 'The silver Eel is bred by generation, but not by spawning as other fish do; but that her brood come alive from her, being then little live eels no bigger nor longer than a pin; and I have had too many testimonies of this to doubt the truth of it myself.'

Sometimes, old Izaak would fall for the three-card trick.

Don't Forget to Write . . .

There Was This Elephant, You See

Though anglers are a peaceful and law-abiding group of citizens, the laws of chance dictate that occasionally one will fall foul of the constabulary. What is recommended is absolute frankness and honesty: tell the truth and fear no man. If that fails, as it usually does, lie through your teeth.

This specimen letter shows how to answer a summons with the absolute truth, for all the good it'll do.

It *is* the truth, too: the elephant and breathalyser incident actually happened to a visitor to a British safari park.

Guilty. Next case . . .

The Clerk of the Court,
Sludgethorpe Magistrates,
Brick Kiln Lane,
Sludgethorpe.

Dear Sir,
I am in receipt of a summons to appear before Sludgethorpe Magistrates' Court next Monday, accused of driving under the influence of drink.

I did attempt to explain the circumstances to the police officer when he breathalysed me, but his only reaction was to ask me to pull the other one, as it had bells on. I found his attitude most unhelpful.

Though in all conscience I have to plead guilty to the charge, I should like to offer the following explanation in mitigation:

I had been fishing the lake in Sludgethorpe Heights Safari Park and had retired to my car for lunch. An elephant approached and started banging on the car roof with its trunk. Out of the goodness of my heart, and in the hope that it would go away, I gave it one of my sandwiches through the open window.

Not content with one, the beast kept sticking its trunk back into the car and pestering for more. I wound up the window to prevent this, and unfortunately trapped the end of the trunk.

The elephant responded by kicking in the wing of the car and sitting on the bonnet, buckling it severely.

I was rescued by the game warden, who shooed the elephant away and then took me to his cabin, where he gave me a little something for my nerves. I readily admit that I took several little somethings before I felt well enough to drive away.

I was almost home when I was stopped by the officer, who wanted an explanation for the state of the car. I told him, perfectly truthfully, that I had been fishing, and that during my lunchbreak an elephant had come along and sat on the car.

At that point, he asked me to blow into the little bag.

Yours sincerely,
Charles J. Chuckerbutty
(Life Member, Sludgethorpe Waltonians Angling Club)

Traditional Angling Techniques

Feeling in the holes under the bank for crayfish to use as chub bait. And discovering that you've got your hand in a rat hole.

Don't worry. Just remember to keep the finger.

It's a Fact

Nourishing Eeel

The eel's flesh has the highest calorie count of any freshwater fish: 1,635 to the pound. No freshwater fish, apart from the salmon, has more than 500. And even the highly nutritious salmon comes a poor second to the eel with 1,173.

It's a Fact

Babs Nabbed 'Em

In August 1975 the British catch record was broken with 304 fish in three and a half hours . . . by a woman.

Mrs Barbara Wilkinson, twenty-three, won the Hawkshaw women's angling championships at Hedon, near Hull. She was persuaded to compete by her farmer husband, borrowed a rod from him and used maggot as bait. As well as the cup for most fish caught, she won trophies for the greatest weight (12 lb 3½ oz) and for landing the biggest roach of the day.

Spectators who wandered from the bank muttering, 'Makes you spit,' were understood to be male chauvinist pigs.

. . . Big bags of fish are easy to come by in Japanese cities where, on Saturday nights, municipal swimming pools are filled with fresh water and stocked with thousands of fish. The anglers gather round the pool shoulder to shoulder, and haul out the fish in double-quick time.

The rumbling noise is Izaak Walton, spinning in his grave.

It's a Fact

Clean Father Thames

The dirty old River Thames is now the clean old River Thames. So clean, in fact, that the salmon have come back to it. The first one turned up in 1974 – before that there had been none since 1833 – and the first was caught on rod and line in August 1983.

It wasn't a big one – 6 lb 12 oz – and it didn't put up much of a fight. 'Knackered,' was how its captor, forty-six-year-old Russell Doig described it. But it was still an historic capture.

The Thames is now the cleanest metropolitan river in the world, with 104 species of fish identified since the great clean-up by the Thames Water Authority.

Clean as the river is, though, an actor in the 1985 series of the ITV London police drama *The Bill* had to have the appropriate injections before he was allowed to fall in the water from a police launch.

Well, you can't be too careful, can you?

Hints for Club Officials

Failure to obey the Seaway Code can cause ill-feeling among fellow anglers.

Confucius he say,
Fingers last longer
If kept out of conger.

Knock, knock.
Who's there?
Lionel.
Lionel who?
Lionel get you nowhere – we all saw the size of your fish.

Knock, knock.
Who's there?
Moira.
Moira who?
Moira fish this canal, Moira think I'm wasting my time.

Knock, knock.
Who's there?
Thayer.
Thayer who?
Thayer thorry for thtepping on my thandwiches.

Knock, knock.
Who's there?
Lettice.
Lettice who?
Lettice have a couple of worms – I'm right out of bait.

Knock, knock.
Who's there?
Justice.
Justice who?
Justice I thought – not a fish in the stretch.

The Angler's Guide to September

Towards the end of September – the twenty-third to be precise – the year moves into Autumn, probably the best all-round time of the year for coarse fishermen. All the fish are in condition and have settled down in their traditional haunts.

With a bit of luck the weather will still be mild and the days not yet too short.

The barbel comes into its own in September, and as a fighter there's no coarse fish to touch it. It hugs the bottom in fast-flowing, gravelly runs, and its flat-bellied triangular shape means that it gets all the help it needs from the current.

Angling for barbel carries another hazard, apart from the fish's ability to break tackle: that of the old boy who wanders up and witters on about the old days when they used to tip in huge sackfuls of worms as groundbait. Ah, he remembers it well.

Tipping in sackfuls of worms is a method that went out with World War One. They couldn't get the chaps any more, for some reason. So unless the old boy really is a trainee corpse and tottering about on two sticks, he's an old fibber who's hoping for a free pint on the strength of his reminiscences. Buy him a pint by all means, but don't let him tap you up for two.

September is also the time for the biggest match event in the coarse fishing year: the annual World Championships. The match is fished in a different country every year. Or if the same country crops up more than once, at least at a different venue.

In 1985 the England team won for the first time since the competition began in 1957. Dave Roper took the individual title, the sixth Englishman to do so.

The World Championships ... What a chance to demonstrate that the true Brotherhood of the Angle knows no frontiers. To show that anglers the world over are one and the same. To live up to the avowed intent of promoting good fellowship among anglers of whatever nation, religion, colour or creed.

What a chance ...

Most years there have been complaints by visiting teams about blatant gamesmanship by the host country. In 1971 in Italy, local anglers talked visiting teams into believing that the only way of catching big fish on the Mincio Canal (near Peschiera del Garda, in case you didn't know) was to use sweetcorn. The foreign (i.e. non-Italian) teams were chucking in sweetcorn by the gallon, which was gobbled up gratefully by the smaller fish. Meantime, the bigger fish were taking maggots. As used by the Italians, who walked away with the match.

In 1976, the venue was Bulgaria. Visiting teams were refused practice near the match stretch and were sent to the other end of the fishery. There were very few bites there because there were very few fish: they'd all been lured into the match length near the dam at Varna by constant feeding.

Not that it did the Bulgarians any good. The Italians cottoned on, snatched the small fish on maggots, and pushed the silly Bulgars into second place.

In 1978 there were complaints about the Austrians. They insisted on keepnets instead of plastic bags. And then dished out keepnets to visiting competitors with mesh big enough to allow most of the tiddlers to swim straight through.

In 1979 the Spanish hosts tried to do things properly. They stocked the Zaragoza Canal with 5,000,000 fish, and threw hundredweights of maize in the water to keep them there. They also strung electrodes across both ends of the match length. Seemed a good idea at the time.

But they left the electrodes switched off until the day of the match. By which time the maize had turned sour and most of the fish had cleared off. If any of the fish tried to get back for the fresh groundbait being chucked in, they couldn't: the underwater electric fence was stopping them, and the result was the lowest weights ever.

Governing body of the World Championships is the Confederation Internationale de la Pêche Sportive – CIPS for short – and they have often been accused of laying down rules which suit continental-style fishing to the detriment of the Angles and Saxons.

But the CIPS complained strongly about English gamesmanship during a heated debate on rule changes in 1974. Back in 1966, they said, the dastardly English had tried the old three-card trick during the international match on the Thurne. Giving visiting competitors nets with large meshes but using small-mesh nets themselves.

There was worse to come. 'Some teams,' said match committee secretary Johs Kleinberg, 'were reduced to asking their ladies for their stockings in order to retain their fish safely.'

A likely story. Asking their ladies for their stockings to keep fish in.

Any excuse, those continental swine. Sex mad, they are ...

> Confucius he say,
> Chippy better for dinner
> Than banking on spinner

It's a Date

September 1

St Fiacre was a seventh-century hermit, born in Ireland but living most of his life in France. He has nothing to do with fishing as such, though he ran a well-tended allotment (his emblem is a spade) and was doubtless good for the odd can of lobs. He also ran a hospice for travellers and eventually became the patron saint of sufferers from haemorrhoids.

As the dreaded piles are one of the many afflictions that angling is heir to, you could do worse than have a quiet word with St Fiacre next time you feel an attack coming on. September 1, his feast day, is a good time for it.

No Sex, Please, We're Anglers

Dedicated coarse anglers should refrain from sex at least a week before and a week after September 16. Otherwise the arrival of the resulting offspring could mess up the first day of next year's new season.

September 30

Last day of the trout fishing season in England and Wales. In Scotland you can fish on until October 6.

The close season includes sea trout but excludes rainbows. You can fish for those until November 15. Dates can also vary from district to district. Just to stop things getting too easy.

Knock, knock.
Who's there?
Chester.
Chester who?
Chester perch and a couple of gudgeon. How've you done?

It's a Fact

Littery Lions

Four British anglers, fishing in a safari park, spent the night locked in their van after spotting what appeared to be lions sitting around outside. The lions sat there all night, not moving a muscle, until the first light of dawn revealed the reason – they weren't lions, they were litter bins.

An angler fishing at the stately home of Longleat was intrigued by a disturbance in the water which was moving slowly towards the bank. Thinking it might be a bream shoal, he moved along the bank to await its arrival. But he didn't stick around when a hippo walked out of the water.

It's a Fact

Keeping It Brief

What for a long time was the longest recorded letter to an editor was written in 1884 to R. B. Marston, editor of the *Fishing Gazette*. It was 13,000 words long and was published in 7 pt type (7 pt type means this size) over two issues.

The correspondent's initials, or pseudonym, were A.R.I.E.L.

It's one of those fascinating facts that you wish you'd never discovered. There's always somebody who asks, 'What did he say, then?'

What *did* he say, then?

He started his letter, 'Sir,' and ended with 'Yours faithfully'. The bit in between was pretty boring.

A.R.I.E.L.'s letter was out-waffled in 1979 by one from John Sultzbaugh to the *Upper Dauphin Sentinel*, Pennsylvania, USA. It was 25,513 words long and had to be published over eight issues.

What did *he* say, then?

Whatever it was, it had nothing to do with fishing.

Traditional Angling Techniques

Sitting on a cold, damp rock for longer than you should and discovering that (a) you can't get up, and (b) your piles are coming on again.

I Say, I Say, I Say . . .

A little boy was sitting on the pavement, fishing in a bucket.

Along came the vicar, took pity on the simple wee soul and gave him 10 p.

'And how many have you caught today, young man?' he asked, patting him on the head.

'You're the fourth,' said the little lad.

The Things They Said . . .

Keep It Shut

> No human being, however great, or powerful, was ever so free as a fish.
>> *John Ruskin (1819–1900)*

Until the fish opened its big mouth . . .

Two And Two Make – Er . . .

> Angling may be said to be so like the mathematics that it can never be fully learnt.
>
>> *Izaak Walton (1593–1683)*
>> *The Compleat Angler*

And the way some people fish, they've never even passed their O-Levels.

Know Your Fish

Barbel (*Barbus barbus*)

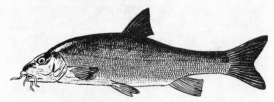

According to the book:
Green or bronze in colour. Likes deep, strong-flowing water. Its dorsal fin carries a saw-toothed spine. Takes wide variety of baits: worms, bread, cheese, silkweed, crayfish, sausage, deadbaits. Moody feeder, strong fighter.
Record: 13 lb 12 oz (6.237 kg)
Between ourselves:
The barbel scoffs any amount of loose feed and ignores your hook bait. The bait it takes is that offered by the bloke who moves into your swim five minutes after you've left. When hooked, the barbel heads for the nearest rock and smashes you. Its dorsal spine, not always apparent as the leading edge of the fin, can be recognised by the stabbing pain in your palm.

Rudd (*Scardinius erythrophthalmus*)

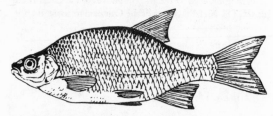

According to the book:
The rudd is a fancied contestant with the grayling for the title of Britain's most beautiful fish. Looks like the more glamorous sister of the roach; bulkier, with bolder face, pugnacious jaw, scarlet fins and bright red eyes. Weight for length, the heaviest British freshwater fish. A surface-feeding shoal fish of slow or still water. Baits as for roach. Classic groundbait is floating crust, anchored by string to a stone.
Record: 4 lb 10 oz (2.097 kg)

Between ourselves:
Like the roach, the rudd is hard to knock. In fact it's got more to recommend it, being the Dolly Parton of the underwater world: buxom, extrovert and highly colourful. Often a saviour on hot days when other fish have lost interest.

I Say, I Say, I Say . . .

A fisherman loaded down with baskets, rods and all sorts of paraphernalia, was trying to get on a bus.
   'You can't come on here with that lot,' said the conductor, and rang the bell.
   As the bus pulled away the angler shouted, 'You know what you can do with your flaming bus, don't you?'
   'Yes,' said the conductor. 'And if you could have done it with all that gear, I'd have let you on.'

Knock, knock.
Who's there?
Guinevere.
Guinevere who?
Guinevere going to catch any fish?

It's a Fact

Small Is Unpronounceable

When you're fishing in Hawaii, think big if you want to be understood. One of the largest local fish is called simply O. One of the smallest is named *Homomomomonukunukuaguk*.
   You could run into tongue-twister trouble, too, by looking for a lake in Massachusetts under its Indian name. The lake is called *Chargogatmanchaugagochaubunagungamaug*, which means 'You fish on your side, we fish on our side, nobody fishes in the middle'. Might be better to ask for it under its English name: Lake Webster.

Know Your Tackle

Hooks

Hooks come in three basic shapes: round bend, which has a bend which is round; crystal, which has a sharper bend; and model perfect, in which the point is offset to make it easier for the hook to penetrate an angler's finger.

Coarse fishing hooks are measured by the Redditch Scale, in which the smaller the number, the bigger the hook. Until you get down to 1, that is, after which, with the addition of the figure 'o', the bigger the number, the bigger the hook.

A scale used by trout fishermen is the Pennell or New Scale. This starts for some reason with 000, then goes on to 00, 0, 1, 2 etc. Because this is much simpler and more logical than the Redditch Scale, the majority of anglers refuse to use it.

The use of barbless hooks has increased greatly of recent years, making it much easier to lose a fish and get a hook out of your ear. Getting a barbed hook out of your ear is a little trickier, but still basically simple.

It is obviously painful to pull the hook out against the barb, so you push it right through until the point comes out at the other side. You then cut the hook through the shank and, with a merry laugh, pull it clean out. Points are lost for yelling, screaming, blubbing, leaping about the bank or other such carryings-on.

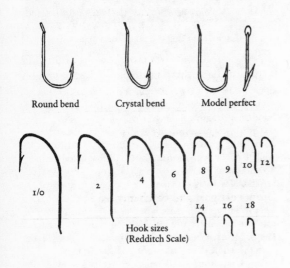

Round bend   Crystal bend   Model perfect

1/0   2   4   6   8   9   10   12   14   16   18

Hook sizes
(Redditch Scale)

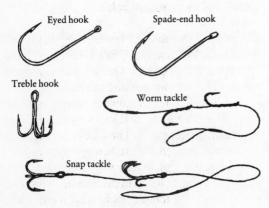

Eyed hook   Spade-end hook

Treble hook

Worm tackle

Snap tackle

Almost all you need to know about hooks. Any questions?

A shell hook used by the ancient natives of the Californian coast. The ancient natives of the Californian coast did not catch many fish.

It's a Fact

The Vanishing Burbot

Anglers have been asked to help in the hunt for the burbot, a rare freshwater cod which was last seen in Britain in 1977. One of the biggest British burbot was the 8 lb specimen caught in the Trent more than 100 years ago (European specimens can weigh 20 lb or more). The one caught in 1977, from a stream near King's Lynn in Norfolk, was a tiddler of only 4 oz.

Great Angling Traditions

Getting Into The Habit

For the monks of old, Friday was fish day. So Thursday was carp day. Down to the old stewpond, get the rods out, and whop in a few of those carp or there's no tea for us tomorrow, lads.

Some of the church elders, mind you, were not in favour of monks going fishing. They came back with such filthy habits. (Jokes like that we can do without. This is serious.)

This rare hand-painted photograph of monks intent on the catch is divided recognisably into the three main attitudes of any group of anglers and demonstrates how little things have changed.

Those in the group on the left are snoozing, scratching, praying or wittering, taking no notice at all of the happenings around them. They may have drawn the duff pegs, or be suffering from last night's overdose of Benedictine cough syrup, but such behaviour is inexcusable among serious fishermen.

The group in the middle is something like. Brother Bighead has hooked a carp and is playing it back to the bank. His technique leaves a bit to be desired: his left hand should be further down the butt, for a start. But he's doing all right. Smirking too much for a man who has renounced the world, the flesh and draught bitter, but still doing all right.

The brothers on either side of Brother Bighead have done the decent thing and grounded their rods. One is saying, 'Gently does it. Don't panic.' The other is holding hand on heart and thinking, 'No chance.'

The biggest responsibility of all rests with the ancient holding the landing net. He's looking very worried. As well he might, with the fish close to the bank and the net nowhere near the water. Down a bit, you silly old fool . . .

Which leaves us with the three brothers on the right. One is looking sideways and muttering, *sotto voce*, 'Jammy bugger'. The next is hoping that the fish is landed safely so he can keep his job. He's the friar. (The fish friar. Get it? Never mind.) The third lad is mightily brassed off with the whole thing – as can be deduced from his recumbent posture – and longing to get back to his psalter. That's his job at the monastery: putting the psalter 'n vinegar on the chips.

After which excruciating and long-dead joke, what can you say? Except thank you. Goodnight. And amen.

The Things They Said

Thanks a Bunch

You should have been here last week. The fish were giving themselves up.
The last bloke you meet on holiday after a fishless week

The Whole Point

It's the utter futility of the whole thing which is its principal appeal.
Angling school principal Colonel Esmond Drury (quoted 1965)

I Say, I Say, I Say . . .

Sid was showing his pal his holiday snaps. One was of his wife holding a hideous-looking angler fish.

'Just look at that,' he said. 'Horrible great ugly thing.'

'Right,' said his pal. 'But what's that she's holding?'

I Say, I Say, I Say . . .

Dopy Alec went shark fishing. When the boat came back he was rushed straight to hospital.

'What happened?' asked a man on the quayside.

'Alec caught a shark,' explained his mate. 'And instead of gaffing it to bring it in, he stuck his arm right down its throat. By heck, they won't call him Dopy any more after this.'

'No? What will they call him?'

'Lefty.'

Who Runs the Club?

The Trophy Custodian

This is a gentle job, ideal for an older member who finds the strain of committee work (i.e. having to stay behind every night drinking after hours) too much for him. Or for some old boy who's making a nuisance of himself and has to be found something harmless to do.

Not that the job is without its responsibilities. Indeed no. In the trophies lies the record of the glory and achievements of the club, and their maintenance and safekeeping is of the utmost importance.

His first job is to get a list of all the trophies from the freshwater captain and the sea commodore. His second job is to find out where the trophies are, to rescue them from prizewinners reluctant to let them go, or to redeem the pawn tickets of those who were less reluctant to let them go.

He is responsible for restoring the trophies to their original condition, which is not always easy with cups that have been used for twelve months as a flower vase, toothbrush holder, dog bowl, door stop or emergency potty.

Any repairs should be carried out by a qualified silversmith, no matter how much the custodian prides himself on his skills with a soldering iron, contact adhesive or carpet tacks.

Polishing the cups is a boring and arduous task and is usually given to the wife.

The custodian's spelling should be impeccable and double-checked. It takes some of the glory away from a prizewinner when he is presented with a trophy on which his name is wrong. It has been known for even the name of the fish to be mis-spelt, with the carp holding the record for transpositions. Few specimen hunters are happy to display a cup, however handsome, inscribed *Crap of the Year*.

The custodian's big moment comes with the approach of the annual prize-giving, when each trophy must be tagged with the recipient's name and the nature of the award. This is to help the luminary presenting the prizes who, by the time the ceremony comes round, is having difficulty in focusing if not in standing up.

At the tagging stage it is often discovered that two cups have been awarded for the same achievement. The procedure here is to re-allocate one of them by a vote at a general meeting. Before this, however, the donor should be approached for his consent.

This is only a formality. The donor's reply is usually predictable enough. 'No you can't,' he says. 'Let the other bugger do it.'

Security of the trophies is all-important. In a big club their value could run into four figures (i.e. £10.27). So it is essential that they are fully insured and kept safely under lock and key, not just chucked in the cupboard with the bingo tickets.

Another task is to review the range of cups every year and recommend re-allocations or the provision of new trophies to make sure that everybody gets a prize. Such awards as *The Dry Net Rosebowl*, *Wally of the Season* and *Pillock of the Year* cause gales of laughter at the presentation and lead to quite lively outbreaks of fisticuffs.

A final responsibility is to persuade retiring club officials to donate a trophy in their own name, which most are happy to do. Anyone too modest or too mean to want to do so can often be cajoled into it by the custodian's long and specialised knowledge of club affairs.

'I just thought a new trophy would make up for the members' concern at the mysterious disappearance of the social club funds last Christmas,' he tells the outgoing treasurer.

After that, all that needs to be settled is the wording of the inscription.

Your Luck in the Stars

Libra (*September 24–October 23*)

'Oo's a pretty boy, then?

There's always one in every club: the bloke who turns up at the water dressed in the height of sporting fashion, spick-and-span from head to toe, looking as if he ought to be on the cover of *Tailor and Cutter*.

However wet the day, however muddy the bank, however many slimy bream he handles, he stays neat and tidy. He is often produced as a typical member to visiting dignitaries, while the really typical members are locked in the tackle shed.

On the club photograph, among all the scruffy, unshaven, grubby, toothless and tatty Neanderthals who constitute the average membership, he stands out like a beacon of sartorial elegance and graceful deportment. An example to us all.

This gets right up the noses of other members because their wives notice and start nagging: 'Why can't you come home looking smart like he does, instead of looking as if the cat's dragged you in?'

'Bloody ponce,' mutter the other members. And make a mental note to shove him in the water next time out.

Poor old Libra, he can't help it: an appreciation of beauty and harmony is part of his nature, so naturally he turns out looking good.

With the sign of the scales indicating a desire for balance, he would appear on the surface to be ideal for conducting the weigh-in. But he can't stand anything that is dirty, disharmonious or violent, which is how most weigh-ins tend to end up.

Like Pisces, he's indecisive, so that would rule him out too. No instant judgments from him. And though he's good at patching up quarrels, he tries too hard to please everybody, so the weigh-in could go on all night. All in all, he's better out of the way, posing for angling fashion pictures in the glossy magazines.

Because of his dislike of mess, his low boredom threshold and his aesthetic leanings, Libra prefers fly fishing to any other form. What's more, it gives him the chance to wear clothes even more upmarket, not to mention a dashing tweed hat covered in highly coloured and totally useless flies.

He's got an idle streak, too, which helps to keep him clean and tidy by avoiding anything too strenuous. A call for volunteers for weed clearance will see him suddenly remembering a previous engagement or having an instant attack of the vapours. Delicate constitution, you see; especially when there's work about. If he *is* roped in, he's the one on the bank dispensing words of advice and encouragement after Leo's gone to the pub.

He's no slouch when it comes to women,

though. Randy as Scorpio, he is, though much better looking. Always ready to take the bait off his hook, sling the line back in the water, and dive into the undergrowth for a bit of nature study. Like Scorpio, too – and Taurus – he's often a candidate on Ladies' Night for having his parting disarranged by a chair wielded by a jealous husband.

He has a smooth line in talk, and in an argument stays pleasant and smiling. He can tell a fellow angler that he's a maggot-brained, cack-handed twit who couldn't catch a starving piranha in a bucket and get the reply, 'Hey, thanks. Nice of you to say so. But I've never claimed to be that good . . .'

His sensual streak often makes Libra overdo the food and drink, but even smashed out of his mind he stays upright and tidy. As the landlord tries to clear the comatose clubmen out of his pub at chucking-out time, Libra can say convincingly, 'My dear chap, I'm not nearly so think as you drunk I am,' and get served with another large Scotch ten minutes after the bell has gone.

Pleasant and agreeable though he is, his indecisiveness and bone idleness do not make him exactly top-flight match material. Match captains wishing to weed out undesirables have one sure method of spotting a Libran: for some reason they all have dimples on their knees. But can you see the average match captain asking a potential team member to roll up his trousers? With all the other lads looking on and muttering: 'So it's true what we reckoned, then?'

Fishing Through The Ages

To Make A Fish-Alluring Ointment

Take Man Fat and Cats Fat, of each half an
ounce, Mummy finely powdered . . .
                    James Chetham
          Anglers' Vade Mecum (1681)

. . . and then, presumably, throw up.

It's a Fact

Bigger Than Both Of Them

In September 1984, Fred Lloyd and Thomas Clark were enjoying some peaceful fishing and a bit of socialising in their 22 ft boat a few miles out from Salcombe, Devon. They had lowered a kedge anchor[1] which dangled 30 ft down and allowed them to drift gently with the tide.

The socialising was with a bunch of skin-divers who had pulled up alongside in their rubber boat to pass the time of day.

Suddenly it all had to stop. Fred and Tom's boat shot off at high speed for 250 yards, leaving the skin-divers behind. Then the bows started dipping, pulling the boat down. Something very big and very fast had caught the anchor.

Both lads sawed at the anchor rope with their trusty knives, and it parted just as the boat was about to go under.

'A submarine,' said Tom. 'We're both certain it was a submarine.'

Let's just hope it was one of ours.

Exactly a year later – September 1985 – and in the same area, Bert Shepherd was in no doubt what pulled his dinghy 3 miles out to sea. It was a giant turtle, which experts thought must have lost its way from the tropics.

Bert had just cast out when the turtle got a flipper tangled in the anchor rope. It swam off in a panic, taking the dinghy and Bert with it at a steady 5 knots. Another boat angler saw Bert's plight, pulled alongside, and grabbed the rope – but the turtle just pulled both boats along.

Finally, 3 miles offshore, it broke free, leaving Bert with a one-that-got-away story worth any amount of fish.

---

[1] Kedge anchor. A small anchor used to keep a ship steady when riding in moving water. Comes from the Icelandic *kaggi*, a keg or cask. The old Icelanders knew what to do with their empties.

The Angler's Guide to October

October can be the golden month for the angler. With the leaves in all their Autumn glory still on the trees and not fouling the water, the weather hopefully unbroken and all the fish in good fighting form, there's not a lot more you can ask.

It's a sad time for the trout man, of course, who has to give up pursuit of the brownies and sea trout from October 1 in England and Wales, and from October 7 in Scotland. But he can still go after the rainbows in most areas up to the middle of November and, if he gets the chance, after salmon until the end of October.

If he's not too snooty about it, he can go fly fishing for grayling. Although a member of the salmon family its season is that of the coarse fish, and in October it's in beautiful condition. Have a go, lad. You could be pleasantly surprised.

As June is traditionally tench time, so October is pike time. Many serious pike anglers, with more self-control than most of us, will not fish for pike before October. Some water authorities, indeed, extend the coarse close season and allow pike fishing only after October 1.

There's a good reason for it. The summer pike is often a mess; skinny but flabby, and clapped out from spawning. Perhaps October is stretching the close season a bit far, but certainly by then the pike has no excuse for not putting up a fight.

Even a medium-sized pike in good fettle is a formidable opponent, and by the time it's thrown itself out of the water a few times, with that great head jagging from side to side, the angler has been given his money's worth. By the time it's on the bank, with that cruel mouth snapping and those eyes looking straight at you, the angler could be forgiven for wishing he's stayed at home.

But it's no excuse for the inexpert bashing to death so often inflicted on pike. It's only a fish, dammit, and out of water at that. A pair of protective gloves, a proper pike disgorger – and a mate to help you if there's one around that isn't chicken – and the hooks can be removed from even the biggest pike with no damage done on either side.

Here endeth the lesson . . .

The Things They Said . . .

Eye, Eye – Whoops!

He [the giant pike] was remorseless, disillusioned, predatory, fierce, pitiless – but his great jewel of an eye was that of a stricken deer, large, fearful, sensitive and full of griefs. He made no movement but looked upon them with his bitter eye.

> *T. H. White (1906–1964)*
> *The Once and Future King*

So next time you catch a pike, make sure you take notice of its beautiful eyes. But mind your fingers . . .

It's a Date

October 28

If you've drawn a duff peg, the weather's playing every dirty trick it can think of and the fish don't wish to know, you could do worse than have a quick word with St Jude, especially on his feast day of October 28.

He's the patron saint of hopeless cases and seemingly lost causes, so if you've been a good lad lately he might send you a nibble or two.

October 31

Last day of the salmon fishing season in England and Wales. Roughly the same in Scotland, but it varies from district to district. Best sources of information are the fishing hotels: the tourist boards seem to find it as confusing as the rest of us.

Know Your Fish

Catfish (*Siluris glanis*)

According to the book:
The Danubian catfish, or *Wels*, was imported in the late nineteenth century to a lake at Woburn Abbey, Bedfordshire. It has spread since to the adjoining counties of Buckinghamshire and Hertfordshire. Likes still or slow water and plenty of mud. Takes worms, bread cheese, deadbaits and offal. Strikes quickly and fights hard. Not a good-looking fish.
Record: 43 lb 8 oz (19.73 kg)

Between ourselves:
That great big mouth, those waving whiskers, those evil little piggy eyes: it's like an unexpected visit from the mother-in-law. Whops away the float and nearly pulls your arms off. When it surfaces, you wish you'd never bothered. Has a nasty habit of flopping along the bank towards you. Enough to frighten the pants off anybody.

Grayling (*Thymallus thymallus*)

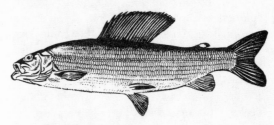

According to the book:
The most beautiful British fish. (OK, there are other contenders, but you can fight it out between yourselves.) Basically silver but shot through with iridescent colours and with a sail-like dorsal fin. A member of the salmon family, it is often scorned by upmarket game fishers and persecuted because of an alleged liking for trout spawn. Has a small mouth, so use hooks 16–20. Takes maggot, wasp grub, grasshopper, small red worms, small spinners, flies and imitation shrimps. A messy, sometimes inaccurate, riser because it often shoots up straight from the bottom.
Record: 3 lb 10 oz (1.644 kg)

Between ourselves:
The grayling is supposed to smell of thyme. To the unromantic nose, it smells a lot like fish. Accused, by anglers who miss on the strike, of having a soft mouth. It doesn't: it has a small mouth, and nips rather than bites. Strikes must be quick, at the first quiver or pluck. Game fishermen who despise the grayling don't know what they're missing. Silly pillocks.

Pike (*Esox lucius*)

According to the book:
Streamlined, ferocious-looking predator found in every kind of water all over the British Isles. Lies in wait and then dashes from cover to seize its prey, which is often a sick or crippled fish. Will also eat frogs, water voles and ducklings, not to mention other pike. Caught on deadbait, spinners or plugs. Livebait, too, if you're that way inclined. Care should be taken in disgorging: the pike has hundreds of teeth, all of which point backwards.
Record: 42 lb (19.05 kg)
Between ourselves:
Perhaps because of its fierce expression and binocular vision – the eyes point straight at you – the pike often brings out the worst in anglers, who kick or bash it to death out of sheer fright. Some angling clubs even encourage this by insisting that pike are not returned to the water after capture. When the last pike has gone, they wonder why they've got a water full of sickly, stunted fish. If nothing else, the pike is bone idle: it would much rather make a short dash for a sick fish than have a lengthy chase after a healthy one. Remember the bit about disgorging: an awful lot of careless pike anglers have trouble with their violin playing.

Knock, knock.
Who's there?
Ivan.
Ivan who?
Ivan ole in my welly.

Knock, knock.
Who's there?
Gopher.
Gopher who?
Gopher the beer – I went last time.

Who Runs the Club?

The Press Officer

Press Officer. It sounds grand, that. Conjures up images of high-level journalistic intrigue; influencing decisions in the corridors of power; mingling with the mighty; slipping high-powered crusading reporters the scoop of a lifetime.

What it boils down to more often than not is discovering the whereabouts of the local reporter and phoning him the results of the evening's match. The latter is often a difficult and lengthy operation because he can't hear you over the noise in the four-ale bar where he's putting back what the day has taken out:

'What's that? Bludgeon? Trudgeon? Dudgeon? Gudgeon! Why didn't you say so? That a fish? How do you spell it?'

However carefully you spell everything out, after the reporter has tried to translate his crumpled and beer-stained notes next morning there's no guarantee that the news will hit the streets in a totally accurate form.

'Prize for the individual weight went to the 2 oz nutter landed by Mr Alfred Gudgeon,' is what appears. '2 oz gudgeon landed by Mr Alfred Nutter,' is what you said. Curses! But at least you tried.

Even the smallest club needs a press officer if it is to get the publicity it needs to build up its membership and have its achievements recognised. Local reporters, though permanently hungry for copy, cannot always spare the time to go chasing after match results, and might not even know that a match has been held. So it's up to the press officer to make life easier for them, to save them having to stir too far from the pub.

Do not be put off from making personal contact by the popular image of a journalist – scruffy, stubble-chinned, chain-smoking, drunken, noisy and brash. Arrange to meet in a pub so that the contact will be friendly and informal, and which the journalist will suggest anyway. Recognition is no problem: just look for someone scruffy, stubble-chinned, chain-smoking, drunken, noisy and brash. Give a firm handshake, a welcoming smile and a warm sincere greeting: 'Miss Jones! So nice to meet you . . .'

Providing the local reporter with match results means that his or her valuable time is not spent attending the match itself. It means also that the results, barring accidents and misprints, are accurate; that impossible demands are not made on the club's hospitality fund; that the reporter doesn't stagger from the match HQ and fall in the water, and that he's not present for the statutory punch-up at the weigh-in.

Your duties include not only supplying information which reflects well on the activities of the club. You must also prevent leaks or rumours which would reflect badly.

'RUNAWAY TREASURER IN CLUBHOUSE LOVE NEST DRAMA' is not the kind of publicity you want to attract, and it is your duty to put the record straight, i.e. flatly deny it.

Do not be too categoric in your denials, though. Do not ring up the reporter and tell him: 'There is absolutely no truth in the scandalous rumour that our treasurer, Mr Herbert Throstlethwaite, 52, of Potbank Terrace, Sludgethorpe, absconded last night with the social club funds and bar takings and is believed to be headed for the Cayman Islands. Nor that he was accompanied by Mrs Lulu Waghorn, 33, of Foundry Road, wife of the former chairman of the veterans' committee, Mr Josiah Waghorn, 73. And certainly no foundation for the scurrilous allegations that Mr Throstlethwaite and Mrs Waghorn have been indulging in anything untoward in the clubhouse broom cupboard after our Wednesday social evenings.'

Should you feel, however, that the situation demands such specific denials, don't waste them on the local reporter. Ring up the nationals and make sure you fix your fee in advance.

Make a special point of inviting the press to the club's important social events, particularly the annual dinner and dance. If there's one thing the average reporter can't resist it's a glittering social occasion such as a free booze-up. Provide him with a list of prizewinners and copies of all the after-dinner speeches beforehand, so that if he nods off or slides under the table he'll have missed none of the side-splitting jokes and pearls of wisdom provided by the speakers.

If any of the speakers has a fatal heart attack in mid-peroration, don't forget to mention this to the reporter when he comes round. He can then phone his news desk like a true professional and say, 'No story on the big speech. The speaker dropped dead.'

Know Your Tackle

Tents, Umbrellas, Windbreaks

The use of a tent, umbrella or windbreak enables the angler to fish longer in inclement weather, and to stay out all night if he so chooses.

There is a theory that many night fishers use the tent for purposes other than just taking shelter, and the windbreak for other than breaking wind. Another school of thought has it that this is merely a malicious rumour, put about by tackle dealers who discover that after an angler has bought a tent, he seldom buys anything more.

Even an umbrella can be used for nefarious purposes. As the Bard so aptly put it:

> There was a young lady of Trent
> Who most inadvisedly spent
> An hour with a feller
> 'Neath his fishing umbrella
> And as good girls go, so she went.

Confucius he say,
Squid bait up nose
Not smell much like rose.

95

Your Luck in the Stars

Scorpio (*October 24 – November 22*)

Know what I mean, John?

Other anglers find it easy to recognise Scorpio on the bank. He's the thickset bloke who turns up at your swim, looking as if he's been thrown out of the inner-city riot squad for brutality, and says:

'Mornin'. I hope you don't think I'm being rude or anything, but I normally fish this stretch. I'd have been here earlier but for a row with the bus conductor. Bloody cheek. Telling me I couldn't take my tackle on board. Still, he'll be all right once they've taken the stitches out.

'Now then. My stretch, right? I'm sure you wouldn't mind moving further down. Nice gear you've got there. Must have cost a bob or two. Shame if anything were to happen to it. Know what I mean, John?'

Life for Scorpio is a constant battle. And there's only one winner: him. He's always right, even when he's wrong. (He's always right *especially* when he's wrong.) He'll argue with anybody, and if there's nobody around he'll argue with himself.

If everyone else is using maggots, he'll use worm and blame his lack of success on the swim, the weather, the cack-handed pillocks fishing either side of him . . . anything but his own bloody-mindedness.

At the weigh-in, he's the first to raise objections about the winner's catch, even though his own 2 oz 3 dms of gudgeon comes nowhere near it. When the winner's claim is finally upheld, he still won't give up. 'See you in the pub car park later, John,' he mutters darkly, breathing on his knuckleduster.

Scorpio takes everything to excess. Sitting at a shallow and silted-up stretch of canal, he'll sling in a half-hundredweight of groundbait for a four-hour match. Souring the swim for the next fortnight unless the ducks can clear it first.

Not that the ducks get much encouragement at his swim, nor any form of animal life for that matter. Dogs he dissuades firmly, though perhaps only temporarily, with a swift clout from the landing net handle. Ducks he dissuades permanently with a swift 'ping!' from his catapult. Go nicely with orange sauce, ducks do.

It's a brave bailiff who books him for fishing without a ticket. And a suicidal one who attempts to confiscate his tackle. 'Here, John. Better take the rod rest first,' says Scorpio. Knotting it expertly around the bailiff's neck.

He's always ready to give advice, asked for or not. He's also very scathing about other anglers' catches, while praising his own efforts to the skies.

'Call that a pike?' he snarls, looking disparagingly at a twenty-five pounder. 'I caught one of twenty inches last week.'

'But lots of people catch pike of twenty inches.'

'Between the eyes?'

His forceful personality would seem to make him ideal match steward material, if it weren't for his habit of skulldragging anglers off their baskets and breaking an arm or two before explaining that they were being disqualified for coughing.

One club position he can take over well is that of secretary, especially if the club is run down and members don't object to its being run like a short-sharp-shock detention centre for very *very* naughty offenders.

If he's not good at book-keeping himself, he soon gets somebody to do it. Or else. He recruits new members by means of gentle persuasion such as blackmail or a knee to the groin, collects all outstanding subscriptions on pain of a broken leg; makes sure the committee men don't get to the bar until *after* they've finished their deliberations, and generally gets the place ticking over.

His methods may not please everybody, but anyone who objects will soon be won round to his way of thinking. There's nothing like a good clogging behind the clubhouse to change a bloke's mind.

. . . Why has this horoscope been written with Scorpio in the third person throughout? Mainly because nobody admits to being a pure Scorpio; you could be born on the cusp with Sagittarius rising or something.

Pure Scorpio . . . Nobody's that bad.

Know what I mean, John?

Great Angling Inventions

The Electric-Powered Floppercopper

An indispensable aid for removing cow dung from the angler's wellies before he enters the house. Note the patented support rail, for use by anglers who arrive home tired and emotional or about to depart from the vertical.

The All-Purpose Correction Chair and Commode

A useful addition to the equipment of any club, this chair can be used in the clubhouse, on the bank, or even in the coach.

Its function is the correction and confinement of:

(a) Club know-alls.

(b) Committee men who won't shut up, even though the bar has been open for a full half hour.

(c) Matchmen who, on the bank, are given to fidgeting, wittering on, bursting into song, whistling through their teeth, bum-scratching, ear-poking or nose-picking.

(d) Club members who, on social nights, will insist on standing on a table and singing *Mother Machree* or reciting revolting rhymes.

The correctee feels no real discomfort, apart from the frustration of being unable to move a muscle. The fact that the chair doubles as a commode means that at least one of his excuses for getting out of it has gone. For the treatment of extreme cases, there's a length of flex and three-point plug at the back.

Traditional Angling Techniques

Slipping in a cowpat. It's easily done and nothing to be ashamed of, especially in the early morning. But later on you are asked to leave the pub and stand in the yard. And you are not very popular with your nearest and dearest when you get home.

Cowpats are fascinating things, in and under which you can find all sorts of creepy-crawlies which make excellent bait. But if you take up the investigation seriously, your social life tends to deteriorate.

Anglers who do wish to study cowpats seriously could do worse than enrol for the special study course, entitled *The Ecology of a Cowpat* (no kidding), at the Preston Mountford Field Study Centre, near Shrewsbury.

A lady student on the six-month course was reported as saying: 'It's quite interesting when you get into it.'

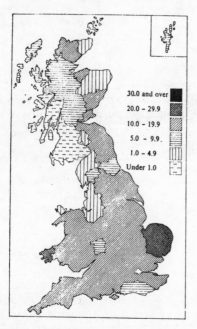

30.0 and over
20.0 – 29.9
10.0 – 19.9
5.0 – 9.9
1.0 – 4.9
Under 1.0

Average daily distribution of cowpats per acre in the British Isles.

I Say, I Say, I Say . . .

The angler's wife visited the Marriage Guidance Council.

'I'm so worried about our relationship,' she told the adviser. 'My Fred stays out all hours fishing, getting home very late and often the worse for wear. I wouldn't care, but when he does get home we always finish up fighting. What can I do about it?'

'A classic case,' said the adviser. 'Very common. He feels unwanted and rejected, that's all. Next time he comes home, put yourself out a bit. Make a special effort. Perfume, make-up, something slinky. Soft lights, sweet music, bottle of wine, Cordon Bleu dinner . . . all that sort of thing. I promise you, it can't go wrong.'

Next time Fred came home, a bit tired and emotional after his team's defeat in the match, he was greeted with just that. His wife kissed him passionately at the front door, stacked his gear under the stairs, took off his anorak and wellies and led him into the dining room. There, the candles were lit, the record player was giving out with soothing music for young lovers, the wine was at exactly the right temperature and from the kitchen came the aroma of a most delicious meal.

After polishing off every last crumb and doing more than justice to the wine, Fred was in a very amiable mood.

'Now then, my love,' said Missis Fred. 'The night is still young. Why don't we go upstairs and I'll slip into something more comfortable. How does that appeal to you?'

'Nothing I'd like better,' said Fred, blissfully. 'But the wife'll kill me when I get in . . .'

Knock, knock.
Who's there?
Havelock.
Havelock who?
Havelock put on your tackle box: you can't trust anyone around here.

It's a Fact

Big Cat

In October 1985 three British anglers were fishing in France in an attempt to break the world carp record when one of them, Londoner John Allen, hooked a 7 ft 6 in catfish (*Wels*) estimated to weigh almost 200 lb (90.72 kg).

After a fight of more than an hour in the big-fish water Lake Cassien, the cat was landed with the help of John's mates, Geoff Shaw and Ritchie McDonald. It had been hooked in 30 ft of water 50 yards from the bank on a 15 lb line, taking a bait of seafood boilies.

The fish had a 13 in mouth and a girth of 40 in, but could not qualify as the biggest freshwater fish ever landed by a Briton because it was impossible to weigh it properly. Scales to hand went to a mere 112 lb, and the fish bumped them down to the limit. There was plenty more where that came from and the fish's full weight was thought to be just short of the 200 lb mark.

The present Hungarian catfish record is 172 lb (78.20 kg). The British record is a measly 43 lb 8 oz (19.73 kg).

You don't get many of these to the pound . . . Captor John Allen needs the help of fellow angler Geoff Shaw to lift the Lake Cassien catfish.

Och, Wumman . . .

A woman was the captor of the British record salmon, taken on Saturday 7 October 1922 from a boat on the River Tay.

Miss Georgina Ballantine was the daughter of James Ballantine, fisherman for Sir Alexander Lyle, Laird of Glendelvine, and her father was rowing the boat for what they had intended as an hour's trolling. The fish was hooked at 6.15 pm and it was two hours later, well after dark, before it was gaffed. Miss Ballantine's arms were swollen from the fight for a fortnight afterwards.

The laird gave the 64 lb fish to Perth Royal Infirmary. Which was jolly decent of him.

Don't Forget to Write . . .

Cash In Hand

Letters to the bank manager lead us into one of the more delicate areas of correspondence, especially when trying to explain the negative state of one's account. Here again, the right approach makes all the difference.

Several points need to be borne in mind:

1. Try to pre-empt a query from the bank manager, i.e. call in or write to explain the situation before he complains to you. This establishes you as frank, open, honest, confident and a bit of a creep.
2. Don't try to be flippant. Bank managers do not have much sense of humour. Especially about money.
3. Remember the bank manager may not be an angler (they tend to go for the more career-oriented sports such as cat strangling and hamster stomping) and therefore may need a detailed explanation of why you're asking for money or why your account is in the state it is. Or both.

. . . The following is a typical letter of explanation sent at the stage where the pre-emption has failed, i.e. when the bank manager has fluffed that the money has not been spent quite as he thought. It's his fault for not acquainting himself better with angling terminology, but the onus is on the poor old angler to get himself out of the nasty.

Mr Adolf Facegrind,
Manager,
National Bouncemunster Bank,
Carey Street,
Sludgethorpe.

Dear Mr Facegrind,
I am in receipt of your communication of yesterday's date, from which I gather you are not entirely satisfied with the state of my account and with the reasons I gave you on my last visit for taking out an overdraft.

If I may take your points in order:

1. It is perfectly true that I needed some of the money to lay in stocks of essential foodstuffs: cheese, bread, sweetcorn, peas, soya meal, bran, flour, custard powder, luncheon meat, frankfurters, liver, bacon and assorted high-protein supplements.
2. It is also perfectly true that I have a wife, four children and two aged parents.
3. I did not say that the foodstuffs were needed for my wife, children or aged parents. I just mentioned my family commitments in passing as a matter of interest.
4. It is true, as you gathered from the local paper account of the Sludgethorpe Waltonians' match prowess this season, that over a period of weeks I have been throwing the aforementioned foodstuffs in the canal. How else do you get the bait to the fish?
5. My project for breeding small livestock, for which I also needed capital, was a genuine one. I may not have mentioned that the livestock consisted of maggots and earthworms, but you did not ask me. You may well have assumed that I meant chickens, rabbits and the odd goat, but with the best will in the world I cannot be held responsible for your assumptions.
6. The investment in capital equipment for a scientific study of the ecology of the local inland waterway system was just that. I bought a new rod and reel as an aid to confirming the distribution and population density of fish species in the canal.
7. The investment in capital equipment for projects approved by the RSPCA for improving the lot of aquatic wildlife was also just that. I bought a new micromesh keepnet and landing net, some non-toxic weights, barbless hooks and a pair of surgical forceps: all aids to the humane treatment of our dumb friends.
8. You query the purchase of pain-killers, sedatives, anti-depressants and peripheral vascular dilators as aids to the health and well-being of myself and others in need of such medicaments, which are not available on National Health prescription.

I freely admit that the money was spent over the bar at the Waltonians' clubhouse and the Bricklayer's Arms. What is draught bitter but a pain-killer, sedative and anti-depressant? And Scotch is the fastest-acting peripheral vascular dilator – in lay terms, a warmer-upper – known to medical science. You should try a day on the canal in the freezing cold and pouring rain without a bite; you would soon realise how necessary are these aids to physical and mental recuperation.

I am sure that from the foregoing you will realise that your initial reaction may have been a little hasty, and that now you are in full possession of the facts you will rest assured that the money was well and wisely disposed of.
Yours sincerely,
Sidney Gungebucket
(Member Sludgethorpe Waltonians A Team)

P.S. Could you please send me one of those trouble-free Personal Loan applications your bank is advertising? As you know, I have a wife, four children and two aged parents.

I Say, I Say, I Say . . .

The landlord of the waterside pub was puzzled by the angler who walked in with a big pike stuck behind his ear, but he decided not to mention it.

'Probably just a show-off,' he thought. 'Just waiting for somebody to ask.'

The next weekend, the angler appeared again with a big pike stuck behind his ear. And the weekend after that, and so on for a couple of months, always with a big pike stuck behind his ear.

(In case anybody is doubting this story, it should be explained that the pike were dead and the angler's ears were whoppers.)

One weekend the angler turned up with an eel behind his ear. The landlord could stand it no longer.

'Don't think I'm being personal,' he said, 'but for a couple of months you've been coming in with a pike stuck behind your ear. And now it's an eel. Would you mind telling me why?'

'Not at all,' said the angler. 'The pike were dead off their feed today.'

Fishing Through The Ages

Real Gone Goose

The principall sport to take a Pike is to take a Goose, or Gander, or Duck, take one of the Pike lines, as I have shewed you before, tie the line under the left wing and over the right wing, as a man weareth his belt, turne the Goose off in a pond where Pikes are, there is no doubt of pleasure betwixt the Goose and the Pike. It is the greatest pleasure that a noble Gentleman in Shropshire giveth his friends for entertainment.

Thomas Barker,
The Art of Angling (1651)

Goosey Goosey Gander,
Whither shall you wander?
Up the pond
And down the pond
And in – Aaaarrrgh!

Cliff Parker,
Rhymes for Sadistic Anglers (1987)

It's a Fact

A Kind of Loving

A forty-one-year-old British angler was tracked down to Rio in October 1985, after his car and tackle were found by the side of a 60 ft deep pool near his home in Bedfordshire.

He'd faked his drowning because of love – too much of it. Friends and fellow anglers subscribed to the theory that his wife looked after him too well, fussed him too much, and that it frightened him off to Brazil.

'I blame myself,' said his attractive thirty-one-year-old wife. 'No man could have been loved more. I fed, bathed and even undressed him when he came home tired out from fishing, although I could never understand his obsession with angling.'

Whether his wife understood him or not, it sounds like every angler's dream of home . . .

Some Incoherent Angling Exclamations and Their Meanings

Events happen so quickly in angling, and are often of such traumatic proportions, that the angler has no time or is in no fit state for detailed explanations.

Here is a short guide for the tourist or non-fisherman to what is meant by some of the commoner angling exclamations:

Aaarrrggghhh!
I have sat on my rod rest.
I have fallen in the water.
I am disgorging a pike and have failed to take the necessary precautions.
I am standing with one leg on the boat and the other on the jetty. The boat is moving away.
I have arrived at the pub to discover that Time has been called.
I am fishing next to an idiot and now have a spinner stuck in my ear/up my nose/somewhere I'd rather not talk about.

Sheesh!
The young lady sunning herself on the opposite bank has rather attractive appurtenances.
I have stuck a hook into my finger in an attempt to impale a bloodworm.
Something huge has just jumped out of the water and flopped back six inches from my float.

This barbed wire fence I am stepping over turns out to be taller than my inside leg.

Yuk!
The herrings I am using as pike bait are not as fresh as when I bought them, which was only a week ago.

Bleargh!
The maggots I was keeping warm under my tongue have disappeared.
The dog that passed this way five minutes ago appears to have done something nasty all over my butties.
I filled my pipe from the maggot tin, in mistake for the tobacco tin which was lying next to it. Wasn't too bad until I inhaled.

Oof!
I misjudged my swing over the top of this stile and am now lying flat on my back.
I sat down rather heavily on my basket, only to discover that the basket's over there.

Whoops!
Cows are very anti-social in their habits and should be more careful about the places they choose for it.

Gurgle Gurgle . . .
I have fallen in the water, surfaced three times and yelled 'Aaarrrggghhh!' at the top of my voice. Nobody has taken a blind bit of notice . . .

Knock, knock.
Who's there?
Paul.
Paul who?
Paul on that rope to get the anchor up.

Knock, knock.
Who's there?
Don.
Don who?
Don fish that swim; it's got my peg number on it.

I Say, I Say, I Say . . .

The captain was playing hell with the duffer of his match team.

'Your record this season couldn't be worse!' he stormed. 'You've got the lowest aggregate in a team of twenty!'

'You'll pardon me,' said the duffer. 'But it could be a lot worse.'

'How?'

'I could have the lowest aggregate in a team of thirty.'

The Angler's Guide to November

What can you say about November?

Except 'Yuk!'

The weather has usually broken into something resembling a bad day in the Yukon; the leaves are off the trees, impeding the floats, clogging the lines, fouling the water and generally putting the fish off their grub; moving water is starting to move faster and creep up higher.

But take heart. The old standbys – the roach, chub and perch – will oblige during the milder spells, should there be any. And the pike still have to eat.

This is the month that sees the last of the fair weather fishermen for a while. They go back to indoor pursuits such as basket weaving and watching naughty videos.

It's also the month that sorts the men out from the boys. Those hardy souls still on the bank, sitting out in the wind, the rain and the sleet are the boys. The men have retired to the pub.

November is also the start of the angling wheezing season. Industrial absenteeism rockets as anglers stay on the bank to fish the last of the light, such as it is, having forgotten to put on an extra set of thermals. Winter draws on, as they say. And if you haven't got your winter drawers on, you're a dead cert for a coughing fit on Monday morning.

Don't forget to take something for your chest, either: goose grease, liberty bodice, extra pully, knitted wool scarf, hairpiece. What many anglers take for their chest is a half bottle of Scotch. Then they wonder why they fall in the water.

Certainly only the most dedicated night fishers will stay on the bank once November sets in. As the Bard put it so well, in a poem dedicated to Chris Binyon and Roy Thomas of the Lucians Specimen Group – a pair of dedicated and intrepid nutcases if ever there were, sitting up night after night through the Winter for pike:

> *When a man grows old*
> *And his hands grow cold*
> *And the end of his nose turns blue,*
> *And he freezes all night*
> *In the hope of a bite,*
> *I'd say he was mad – wouldn't you?*[1]

The Things They Said . . .

Wow!

Fish die belly-upward and rise to the surface; it is their way of falling.

André Gide (1869–1951)

André Gide, French author and philosopher, was noted for his very deep thoughts. This wasn't one of them.

---

[1] For the full text of this stirring epic poem, see *Hook, Line and Stinker* by Cliff Parker (Sphere Books). Any resemblance to *Eskimo Nell* is purely intentional.

Know Your Fish

Perch (*Perca fluviatilis*)

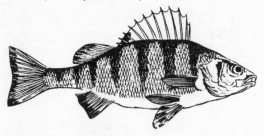

According to the book:
Handsome, dashing fish with green-gold flanks, black zebra stripes and bristling dorsal fin. Bites boldly with bobbing motion of the float. Fighting-bull humped back gives jagging fight. Has large, soft mouth, so needs careful playing. Caught on lob and deadbait, fished sink-and-draw; on spinners and spoons. And on maggots. Not at all fussy.
Record: 5 lb 9 oz (2.523 kg)
Between ourselves:
Though the perch's fight feels spectacular, it's really not all that powerful because of its weak tail. Like the fighting bull, all the strength is in the shoulders. Its first dorsal fin is well armed with spines, as novice anglers discover when they pick the fish up. Always remember to stroke it from the head backwards. There are spines on the other fins, too, and even the gill covers end in sharp spikes. So watch what you're doing. A perch is delicious grilled with butter; knocks spots off your average trout.

Roach (*Rutilus rutilus*)

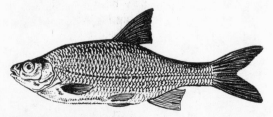

According to the book:
The most common angler's fish in the British Isles. Gentle and shy. Mainly a bottom-feeder with delicate if unexciting colouring. Takes a wide range of small baits: maggots, casters, worms, bread, hemp, wheat, tares and cheese. Goes for natural baits, too, such as caddis and wasp grubs, caterpillars, woodlice, dock grubs, small slugs, elderberries, bloodworms, pieces of swan mussel and silkweed. Fish light on a tip-action rod, and strike quickly.
Record: 4 lb 1 oz (1.842 kg)
Between ourselves:
The roach is such a nice, unassuming fish that it's hard to knock it. It has no bad habits, except perhaps for a tendency to catch nasty diseases now and again. Since its introduction into Ireland at the turn of the century, it has spread there steadily and in places has ousted the native rudd. It's a bit confusing because the rudd in Ireland has always been called the roach. (How *do* they do it? God bless 'em.)

Know Your Tackle

Disgorgers

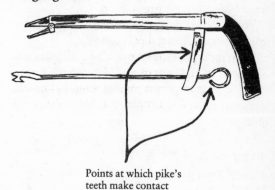

Points at which pike's teeth make contact with your fingers

Two types of pike disgorger.

A disgorger is used to take the hook out of the fish's mouth. The idea is to hold the fish in the left hand and use the disgorger with the right. Unless you're left-handed, in which case forget it. As the fish is flopping madly about, you remember that the disgorger is in an inside pocket under several layers of impenetrable clothing, or somewhere among the jumble at the bottom of the basket.

The simplest type is the *fish-tailed* disgorger, famed for its inaccuracy and inefficiency. Perhaps kinder to the fish and easier to use in cases of watering eyes, pre-pub shakes or post-pub wobblies is the *ring-ended* type which is slid down the line and over the shank of the hook.

Many anglers use *needle-nosed pliers* or *surgical forceps* in preference to traditional disgorgers. These are not only held to be more efficient, but give the whole operation a touch of the Dr Kildares.

Pike disgorgers have extra-long handles. The reason for this is apparent the first time you try to unhook a pike with an extra-short handle.

I Say, I Say, I Say . . .

Harold was in trouble with his wife. He'd forgotten their wedding anniversary and she was in tears at the breakfast table.

'I bet you don't remember one single thing about our wedding day,' she sniffed.

'I do indeed,' said Harold. 'The wedding was at three in the afternoon. That gave me the chance to nip down to the river before the ceremony, and I caught that beautiful 25 lb pike.'

Knock, knock.
Who's there?
Genoa.
Genoa who?
Genoa good bait for this water?

Knock, knock.
Who's there?
Emma.
Emma who?
Emma fraid I fell in the canal, love.

Your Luck in the Stars

Sagittarius (*November 23–December 21*)

Bring on the clown

Quick results are what you're after. No careful planning ahead for a fishing trip, charting the water, mixing secret baits, practising your casting techniques on the lawn. None of that. You just chuck a few things into your beaten-up wicker basket, get down to the water and become impatient when you've not had a bite from the first cast.

But not to worry. You're one of nature's gypsies, a restless wanderer for whom the grass is always greener on the other side of the hill, and the swim around the next bend is always packed with fish. If it isn't, there's always another bend, another swim.

You've an intense curiosity about everything, experimenting with natural baits during the summer and occasionally surprising yourself by hooking a whopper.

To be fair you hook more whoppers than your skills entitle you to. You have the luck of the devil. If someone's been trotting down prime lobworms to a big barbel all morning and finally gone away in disgust, you're the one who turns up next and trots down a scraggy old brandling just as the fish is feeding peckish. But your luck can give out suddenly, such as when the first bloke returns, sees you grassing the barbel that broke his heart, jams your landing net over your head and stuffs the barbel down your trousers. Very spiky, barbel.

Creative though you are, it's no use wasting time trying to make your own floats. It takes patience and attention to detail, neither of which you have. All you finish up with is a collection of bent and cracked monstrosities, a lacerated left thumb and a hefty bill for re-surfacing the dining table.

A well-developed sense of justice and fair play seems to mark you down for club office, especially on the match side. But you're impatient with detail and routine and would be the sloppiest, most disorganised official the club ever had.

And though you're popular with your mates, your natural bluntness doesn't always go down well with strangers. You're lacking in tact, tending to say things like: 'My, you really fished well today. I'd never have suspected that of somebody as thick as you.'

You're a happy-go-lucky bloke, always looking on the bright side of things. If a sudden downpour drives you away from the bank to seek shelter, you console yourself with the thought that if it hadn't been for the rain, you wouldn't be sitting in this cosy little pub.

While the bloke next to you is moaning that he's been fishing all morning and only caught three miserable gudgeon, you take a more positive view. You've been fishing all morning and been lucky enough to catch three splendid gudgeon.

Your sunny nature is part of your other gift: you're a natural clown, often wasting time by larking about when you should be fishing. The clowning increases your accident-proneness, which is almost as bad as Aries'. If there's a lock gate or a jetty to fall off, you'll fall off it; often because you were tap-dancing across the lock or doing handstands on the jetty. If there's a chance that a boat will move away from the landing stage just as you're stepping aboard, it will move away. Leaving you with watering eyes as your resources are overstretched, or pitching you straight into the drink. Often both.

The clowning doesn't fit well into the serious business of match fishing, and you're often disqualified under the no-talking rule for tell-ing the one about the angler and the farmer's daughter; or under the no-moving rule for leaving your basket for a quick song-and-dance routine or a couple of cartwheels.

You are vulnerable in the feet, bowels, hips, liver, lungs, hands, arms and shoulders. Which doesn't leave much else to be vulnerable in. The hazards involved just in getting to the water mean that you often arrive there having fallen off a stile, slipped in a cowpat, been chased by a bull and fallen in the water from a spur of undercut bank. Philosophical as ever, you cheerfully set out your stall and sit down — straight on to your spare rod rest.

You often overdo the Demon Drink, and here both your luck and your accident-proneness come into play. You're lucky enough to have a couple of mates to escort you home; unlucky enough to have them prop you up at the front door, ring the bell and run away. When your wife flings the door open wide, you're accident-prone enough to fall straight through, flat on your face. And that was the only bit that wasn't supposed to be vulnerable.

Who needs teeth, anyway? Only something else to clean. Tomorrow we'll really get the show on the road . . .

Traditional Angling Techniques

Trying to get back to dry land after falling in the water.

Always a tricky operation this, even when you're sober. But when the current's fast, the water's rising, the bottom's shifting and your wellies are full, you can be excused for thinking that you've known better days.

That dog's not much help either, standing there wanting you to throw sticks.

Great Angling Traditions

An unprincipled person about to nick a fellow angler's groundbait.

It's a Fact

Off the Map

You could be disappointed if you try to go fishing in some reservoirs in Oklahoma, USA. They're on the map all right, but funds for them ran out before they could be built.

Inspecting a Spectre

Anglers nightfishing in Buckinghamshire in the seventies were terrified by a 'ghost' – a spectral white shape which flew slowly around in the dark, uttering mournful cries. One of the lads finally plucked up courage and clapped a landing net over it.

It was an owl which had collected phosphorescence on its feathers from the old barn it lived in, making it glow in the dark.

. . . Other anglers in Buckinghamshire are still trying to explain the phantom fisherman they saw one night at dusk. He was sitting further along the bank, large as life. The anglers shouted 'Good evening!' and walked up to see how he was getting on. As they got close, he vanished. Didn't move – just vanished.

Not even the Demon Drink could explain it. The anglers were stone cold sober. At least, that's what they said.

I Say, I Say, I Say . . .

The angler climbed into the railway carriage, soaking wet, covered in mud and slime, smelling of beer, laden with gear and starting to steam: a not unusual condition after a hard day's fishing.

He was met with very stern stares and curling of the top lip from a very haughty young lady sitting opposite.

'Don't let it worry you, love,' he said. 'We lost the match today. I'm committing suicide at the first tunnel . . .'

Who runs the club?

Presidents and Vice Presidents

This is where things get complicated.

A president can be a senior club member, a showbiz personality, an angling personality, a local MP or civic dignitary. He can actually do something for the club or just lend his name to it and turn up only once a year for the annual shindig.

He can be chosen by the committee or elected by all the members. His appointment can be for twelve months, for several years or for life.

The same applies to vice presidents, and the lengthier appointments can mean that the club finishes up with a dozen or so old buffers claiming seniority, pulling rank, crowding the committees, hogging the bar and generally getting in the way.

The offices of president and vice president are believed, in some quarters, to have been thought up by the Dirty Tricks Department of the anti-angling lobby.

. . . old buffers claiming seniority, pulling rank, crowding the committees, hogging the bar and generally getting in the way.

It's a Fact

Man shoots pike – and pike shoots man

Several pike have been caught by unconventional methods in Ireland. One of 61 lb was caught on the River Bann after almost capsizing the angler's boat by biting the oar.

A 64 lb whopper was pitchforked in Lough Derg. And specimens of 39 lb and 53 lb 11 oz were *shot*.

But the pike caught on Lake Manitoba, Canada, by trapper Joe Benoit, got its own back. Joe put the 'dead' pike in the bottom of his canoe. With a flick of its tail it triggered off his rifle and shot him dead.

Knock, knock.
Who's there?
Wilma.
Wilma who?
I've been here all day. Wilma float never dip?

Knock, knock.
Who's there?
Punch.
Punch who?
Punch somebody else – it wasn't me who stepped on your rod.

Confucius he say,
Pike down trousers
Better than piranha in bath.
But probably not much.

Angling Superstitions

Unlucky For Some

The rod-and-line angler shares some of the deep-sea fisherman's superstitions, including the one about its being unlucky to count the catch until the day's fishing is over. If he does, the fish will stop biting, no matter how well they are rising for other anglers.

Many anglers will throw back the first fish of the season if it's female. Nobody's quite sure why, but one possibility is the belief that the female is the weaker sex, and therefore a bad omen for the rest of the season.

Another superstition is that it is unlucky for a fisherman to meet a woman on the way to the water, especially a strange woman or a squinting one. Many an angler discovers the truth of this as he's creeping downstairs in the early morning to be met with a cry of, 'And where do you think you're going? You're not stirring out of this house until you've fixed the washer on that tap!'

The woman may be his nearest and dearest, but at that time of day she's certainly very strange. And if she's squinting as well, he stands no chance.

Knock, knock.
Who's there?
Liza.
Liza who?
Liza what fishermen tell.

It's a Fact

Not So Nasty

There are more than 300 types of shark, but only 75 of them are aggressive towards man. If you don't know which 75 they are, stay out of the water. Only 50 people in the world are killed by sharks every year. Many more people are killed by lightning. Come to that, many more people are killed by bee stings.

In the stomach of a shark caught in the West Indies was a pair of suede shoes, a human skull and a copy of the Gospel According to St John – the only known case of a shark that got religion.

The Wisdom of Angling

When the wind is in the east,
'Tis neither good for man nor beast;
When the wind is in the north,
The skilful fisher goes not forth;
When the wind is in the south,
It blows the bait in the fishes' mouth;
When the wind is in the west,
Then 'tis at the very best.

Old English rhyme
Anon

When the wind be in the east,
T'ain't no good to man nor beast.
And when the wind be in the west,
It blows right up your little vest.

New English rhyme
Cliff Parker

I Say, I Say, I Say . . .

The millionaire was being treated just like any other customer in the tackle shop, and was annoyed that more deference was not being paid to his wealth and social standing. So to make his presence felt, he said to the assistant, 'Just give me maggots to the value of ten pounds.'

'I'm sorry, sir,' said the assistant. 'We don't do the small tins any more.'

'This fish I've caught,' said Jim, 'weighs 25 lb if it's an ounce.'

'Impossible,' said his mate. 'Look, I've got my scales here. Let's try it.'

The fish weighed in at just over 5 lb.

'Would you believe it?' said Jim. 'The bloody thing's hollow!'

The Angler's Guide to December

After the rain, fog, frost and snow of November, it's quite a relief to get to the rain, fog, frost and snow of December. Whatever the weather in December, it doesn't matter.

As is to be expected in the season of goodwill to all men, comfort and joy and the odd spot of ding dong merrily, December is a month devoted to socialising rather than serious fishing. The true Brotherhood of the Angle is expressed in friendly matches and club socials; at the Yuletide Ladies' Night where the anglers' wives can swap barmy-husband stories and commiserate with each other; in the cementing of old friendships and suspension of old rivalries around a log fire in a hospitable fishing pub.

Everybody, in other words, gets wellied.

The effect this has on any attempt at serious fishing is evident at the traditional Boxing Day match. Those matchmen who do turn up bear a strong resemblance to zombies on a bad day; shuffling, stumbling, peering blearily about them and not quite sure where they are or what they're supposed to be doing.

There is a high incidence of hooks in ears and terminal rigs in trees; a fair amount of injury sustained by tripping over baskets, sitting on rod rests and falling in the water.

Neither individual nor team weights qualify for the record books, most of the anglers being fast asleep when the float bobs or the rod tip twitches. The fish, in fact, do very well out of it, scoffing hundredweights of groundbait liberally laced with secret ingredients such as surplus Christmas pudding and high-protein minced parson's noses, and being left to strip the hook baits at their leisure.

Though the catches might be minimal or non-existent, the work of the stewards, captains and match secretaries is greatly increased during a Boxing Day match.

A lot of their time is spent fishing the clumsy and incautious out of the drink. And they have the added responsibility of ensuring that those lads still sitting on their baskets after the final whistle are merely sleeping, and have not passed over from the effects of excess or hypothermia.

True to the spirit of angling, such inconveniences as the odd corpse are not allowed to cast a shadow over the proceedings. To rush straight back home with the dear departed would not only mean some of the lads missing their ale, it would not be fair on the deceased's widow, who would still not have cleared up after Christmas Day.

A defunct angler is carried by his mates into the pub and sat down in a quiet corner. (This causes no comment from the landlord: he's used to seeing Boxing Day anglers sitting stock still with their eyes shut.) And if the angler's got the price of a round on him, he may have the posthumous privilege of buying a last pint for his stalwart comrades.

This is not only the true Brotherhood of the Angle. It's as he would have wished . . .

Traditional Angling Techniques

Admiring the size of the catch while at the same time trying to get the hook out of your thumb during the Boxing Day match.

It's a Date

December 15

Don't forget: Izaak Walton died on 15 December 1683. Dedicated anglers will have a pint or two in his memory, and perhaps add a literary touch to the occasion by indulging in an Izaak Walton epitaph competition.

All you have to do is to compose some appropriate verses for the old lad's tombstone. Best one earns a free pint. To get you going, here are some examples:

> *Here lies Izaak,*
> *Best of the batch.*
> *When the great whistle blew,*
> *He finished the match.*

> *Here lies Izaak.*
> *God rest him.*
> *He's trotted his cork*
> *To the end of the swim.*

> *Here lies Izaak,*
> *Under the sod.*
> *He's packed his gear*
> *And popped his rod.*

And there's always the good old good one:

> *Here lies an honest man*
> *And a dedicated angler.*
> *It's not often they bury them*
> *Both together.*

December 21

December 21, the shortest day in the northern hemisphere, is officially the start of Winter.

Those anglers suffering from waterlogging, hypothermia or double pneumonia can take comfort from the fact that the mist, fog, wind, hail, rain, sleet and snow of the past couple of months have been merely manifestations of Autumn.

You ain't seen nothin' yet. Kof kof . . .

I Say, I Say, I Say . . .

Wife: 'Harold! I know you've been fishing, but look at the state you're in! What *have* you been doing?'

Angler: 'I fell in the water.'

Wife: 'In your new pullover?'

Angler: 'I'm sorry, but there wasn't time to change.'

'Dad, do you know what I'm going to give you for Christmas?'

'No, son. What?'

'A fixed-spool reel that works.'

'That's very nice of you, son, but I've already got a fixed-spool reel that works.'

'Not any more you haven't. I've just trodden on it.'

Confucius he say,
Fishing with wind in face better than
Fishing with frostbite in long johns.

Know Your Tackle

Odds and Sods

These are not exactly essential pieces of tackle or gear, but they are useful things to carry for blokes who like the everything-but-the-kitchen-sink approach to angling and don't mind risking the odd double hernia.

Bite Indicators

These are of several types, beginning with the basic *dough bobbin*. A dough bobbin is a small ball of dough squeezed on to the line. After about ten minutes in the wind it dries out and falls off.

A *swing tip* hangs from the end of the rod on a flexible plastic 'tail'. When a fish bites, the swing tip swings out, drops back or swings sideways. It does the same when the wind blows.

A *target board* is a board with a geometric pattern painted on it. Placed as a background to the swing tip, it protects it from the wind and helps the angler to register the tip's slightest movement. After a while, your eyes go funny.

A *quiver tip* is a tip which quivers. Less affected by the wind, but sometimes quivers merrily in a strong current when there's not a fish for miles.

A *butt bite indicator* is a hinged arm which clips on the bottom joint of the rod with the free end resting against the line. When a fish moves the line, the arm swings upwards. Adds to the general complications when it tangles the line on the reel-in.

An *electric bite alarm* looks like a rod rest with a battery-operated device in place of the fork. When a fish takes, a buzzer sounds and sometimes a light flashes. Used mainly by anglers who hope to hear the buzzer from the public bar, or by night fishers who often switch the thing off so as not to be distracted from the real purpose of the trip out.

Swim feeders and *bait droppers* are used for feeding swims and dropping baits. Excellent for stunning fish and braining inquisitive ducks. Bait droppers have to be retrieved after dropping the bait, leaving the angler hoping he can hit the same spot with his hook bait. Swim feeders are left on the line, have to be used with a short, stiff rod, and the fish hook themselves. Not the most delicate form of fishing known to man.

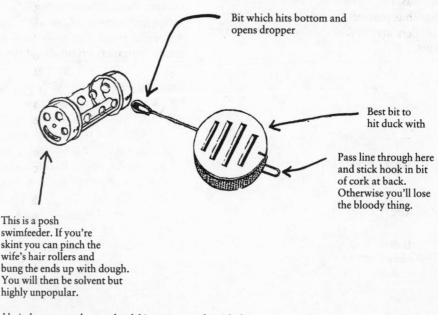

Bit which hits bottom and opens dropper

Best bit to hit duck with

Pass line through here and stick hook in bit of cork at back. Otherwise you'll lose the bloody thing.

This is a posh swimfeeder. If you're skint you can pinch the wife's hair rollers and bung the ends up with dough. You will then be solvent but highly unpopular.

Swim feeder and bait dropper, and a couple of things you can do with them.

Gaff

A big, barbless hook on a long handle, used for landing pike, salmon and sea fish. Its freshwater use is now banned or being phased out in favour of a large landing net: not only is its use not altogether comfortable for the fish, its inexpert handling leads to a lot of perforated anglers.

Polaroid Spectacles

Not only do these cut out glare from the water, they enable the angler to see a fair distance below the surface and so locate the fish. He is then able to cast right under the fishes' noses and spend the rest of the day observing them chomping up his groundbait and totally ignoring his hook bait.

Priest

A weighted cosh for killing fish. Best to buy a heavy one rather than a light one: saves you having to play the *Anvil Chorus* on a big fish, as performed so often by angling experts on the telly, usually as the sun is sinking slowly in the west.

Rod Holdall

This makes the carrying of several rods a lot easier. Has the drawbacks of knocking old ladies off bus platforms and causing farmers to have anglers arrested on suspicion of carrying firearms.

The Things They Said . . .

Fish On Regardless

> The gods do not deduct from man's allotted span the hours spent in fishing.
> *Old Babylonian proverb*

Look younger, live longer – and you're not even doing it in your own time.

Who Runs the Club?

The Patron

The club patron is often a noble lord, upon whose land the members are allowed to fish.

Fishin' – as he pronounces it, having been to a good school with a lousy English master – is somethin' he never practises himself. But he knows it's vaguely akin to huntin' and shootin', of which he does a lot. Akin also to pig stickin', of which his grandpapa was a devotee in the days of the Raj. (Never been the same since we lorst India, pig stickin'.)

Fishin'. Yerss . . . Salmon and trite and all that. Not much you can tell him abite trite fishin'. The old dray flay and all that.

When he inherited his title and estate, he inherited the angling club. He's always been a bit confused about this, but knows it's something his grandpapa would have wished. His grandpapa wished it because he was caught in the long grass in 1910 with the wife of the then club secretary. Ever since, the club has had the right to fish the ancestral waters. Before 1910 the relationship was a little less harmonious, i.e. any angler found in the grounds (sorry: find in the grinds) was shot on sight.

Several times the noble lord has asked his estate manager, grandson of the original club secretary, to look into the possible revenue from the little river which meanders through the estate. Always the answer has been the same: 'No salmon, no trite, your grace. May as well let the hoi polloi amuse themselves in pursuit of the commoner kinds of fish. *Noblesse oblige*, your grace, if you take my meaning.'

The noble lord's name looks good on the club notepaper. And his presence lends a bit of tone to the annual dinner and dance. Though he knows not a soul there, he smiles and nods his way through the proceedings and greets each prizewinner with an aristocratic and patronising, 'Well done. Jolly good', wondering the while what kind of fish a gudgeon might be. Certainly not a breed of trite.

The patron's lady wife often accompanies him to the dinner and dance. She enjoys it not quite so much (i.e. not at all) because she knows even less about fishing than does her husband. And by the time she's had the obligatory dances with the president, six vice presidents and chairman, her feet are killing her. (*Their* feet are killing her, but let's not be pedantic.)

Both lord and lady are introduced to selected members of the club who have been coached in what to say – 'Good evening, your grace', not ''Ow do, cock' – and who have been checked to ensure that they have put their teeth in, combed their hair and are reasonably sober.

It is customary for the patron and his good lady to depart before the end of the proceedings. This means that the club members can relax and enjoy themselves, and also that the noble pair are well clear of the premises before the fighting breaks out.

Your Luck in the Stars

Capricorn (*December 22–January 20*)

Me? Worry?

Don't take this personally. You'll only start worrying again. And you've nothing to worry about, really, except the fact that you're a born worrier. You know you'll get to the top all right. You always do.

Capricorn is methodical, single-minded and, when it comes to the crunch, ruthless. He's the

mad matchman, the ace tiddler-snatcher, flicking the fish out of the water and flicking back a re-baited line almost in a single movement. The fish are incidental: he'd be just as happy hooking cardboard fish on a fairground stall providing there was money in it. It's the cash prize he's after, and he's put in hours of practice at home to make sure he gets it.

His baits? What's that got to do with you? He's spent years experimenting with secret superbaits and he's not going to give the formula to anyone. Find your own flaming baits.

Or he's the specimen hunter, obsessed with one particular fish to the exclusion of all others, steadily working his way through every known technique in single-minded pursuit of his quarry, adapting his tackle and baits until he hits on the right combination and becomes gudgeon-basher of the year.

He takes defeat badly. Not in the physical way of Scorpio, but by going off in a sulk for a while, then coming back with a carefully worked-out plan for getting his own back. Cross Capricorn and he'll get you if it takes ten years. There'll be no nastiness – well, not a lot – no trickery: he'll do it all by the rules and make sure it sticks.

His tackle, like Virgo's, is kept in immaculate condition and perfect repair. Nobody is allowed to borrow it, especially loony Leos and loonier Sagittarians. So you've left your landing net behind, eh? Tough. You'll know better next time.

He's a good organiser, even though he sticks to the letter of the rule book rather than the spirit. Give him a steward's armband, let him loose on the bank, and he'll have everyone disqualified within fifteen minutes.

Give him club office as secretary or treasurer and you'll have the most efficiently run club for miles. It won't be a lot of fun, though. If the book says the bar closes at 10.30, the bar closes at 10.30. No crafty ones after hours, no matter how much his fellow members plead, cajole, weep, wail or attempt to bribe. It's no use even fainting in an attempt to get a brandy. After 10.30 all you'll get is a bucket of water chucked over you.

Capricorn is hardly the life and soul of the club. He's very careful with his money, to start with. If ever he takes out a fiver at the bar, there's a flurried exit of moths and the Queen is left blinking in the light.

He doesn't approve of the Demon Drink, anyway. You can lose control by over-indulgence, and he's not going to lose control. He has his reputation to think of.

His reputation is often that of a misanthropic old miseryguts. Running a club or fishing a match is a serious business. There's no place in it for laughing or larking about. And he can prove it by pointing to Leo, standing sniffling and soaking wet in the pub. Or to Sagittarius, lying on the bank with a broken leg and waiting for the ambulance after cartwheeling straight into a rabbit hole.

Capricorn is constantly on his guard against treachery and deceit. Paranoia, it's known as in the trade. So even if his fellow members make the effort to include him in the line-shooting at the bar, he suspects their motives. They're not making a fuss of him for himself alone. Oh, no. They're trying to draw him out so he'll reveal the formula for his magic groundbait; trying to get him to demonstrate the wrist action that gives him the fastest strike in the club. They're not going to worm his secrets out of him that easily. He wasn't born yesterday.

Whenever he *was* born, he was born middle-aged. In the junior section he's the serious, spotty and bespectacled lad who reads everything about fishing he can lay his hands on, wanders off on his own while the other lads are larking about, and comes back with a netful of fish. He gets home to mother in the same condition as he left: not a speck of mud, not a trace of slime, no cuts, bruises or abrasions. You'd never know he'd been fishing at all.

Is there nothing about Capricorn to soften the austere image, to make him seem more human? Well, he does have a tendency to break out after middle age, to make up for the good times he never had as a youth. This can take the form of a passionate fling, perhaps running off with the chairman's wife.

That's always good for a laugh . . .

Don't Forget to Write . . .

As He Would Have Wished

One of the saddest letters a club secretary has to write is the letter of condolence after a member has gone to the Great Weigh-In in the Sky.

Here, the message must be expressed briefly in sincere and comforting words, with perhaps the addition of some of your own fond memories of the deceased.

Mrs Cyril Higginson,
13 Potbank Close,
Foundry Road,
Sludgethorpe.

Dear Mrs Higginson,
It was with great sadness that I learned of the death of your husband, Cyril.

He was, as you know, a great stalwart of club social nights, and did much to cheer up our members with his recitals of *The Green Eye of the Little Yellow God* and his imitations of James Cagney doing his *Yankee Doodle Dandy* tap-dancing routine.

It must have been some comfort to you, as it was to us, to learn that he was performing the latter when he slipped and fell into the canal from Foundry Road lock, thereby catching the cold which took him from us.

Social nights will never be the same without him; already the bar takings are significantly down.

He will be very much missed by us all.

Yours sincerely,
Eli Witherspoon,
Secretary, Sludgethorpe Waltonians
Angling Club.

P.S. Did he say anything about a match rod?

Knock, knock.
Who's there?
Colin.
Colin who?
Colin in at the pub on the way home?

For The Angler Who Has Everything

Don't delay!!! Order today!!!

Though it is possible to fish quite adequately with a minimum of equipment, enjoyment of the game – not to mention personal comfort and safety – can be enhanced by the odd piece of specialised tackle or clothing. Among the latest additions to the Parker Groovigear Angling Catalogue, ideal for Christmas gifts, are:

Ferret-Proof Long Johns

Equipped with patented double-locked naughty bits protector, these long johns ensure that never again need you fear damage inflicted by ferret or wild mink on the rampage up your trouser legs. Proof also against most flying and crawling insects, nesting mice and hibernating hedgehogs.

Heron-Proof Jockstrap

Made from felt-lined, laser-welded, rustproof titanium, this lightweight jockstrap offers protection against low-flying herons and ill-disposed swans. Absolutely undetectable in use. Worn at peg disputes, match weigh-ins or during heated debates at club AGMs, it helps to cut down the incidence of watering eyes and funny walks.

Knock, knock.
Who's there?
Althea.
Althea who?
You go on ahead. Althea down at the water.

Knock, knock.
Who's there?
Norah.
Norah who?
Norah bite all day.

Knock, knock.
Who's there?
Watson.
Watson who?
Watson your hook? I'm using worms myself.

Superstrength Drinking Braces

Hand-tailored from cross-ply nylon webbing, these braces will take all the strain of a convivial evening, including chest-inflating and braces-twanging during boasting sessions, without ever overstretching or snapping. Never again will you be caught with your trousers down.

Blackhead Extractor and Fish Enhancer

A boon to spotty junior anglers who are allergic to soap and water. Unique vacuum action removes blackheads from nose immediately. Would take hours of fishing into the wind to achieve the same effect.

Used in reverse, pumps up undersized fish to specimen standard in seconds without the risk of chapped lips or fins up the nose.

The Dolly Parton Double-Chamber Micromesh Keepnet and Bloodworm Strainer

Mesh guaranteed so fine that not even a bloodworm can squeeze through. So no more will your catch swim straight through the mesh. And no more will you find the gudgeon gone and the perch burping gratefully: the Dolly Parton Double-Chamber Micromesh Keepnet and Bloodworm Strainer keeps the predators separate from the tiddlers and ensures that everything you catch, you keep. As its name implies, it does double duty by straining bloodworms from the water butt whenever they are needed in quantity. That's what you tell the wife, anyway, when she finds similar objects among your night-fishing gear.

Expandable Hat

Specially designed for the successful angler, the hat expands automatically to the changing size of the head occasioned by the winning of a match, the landing of a specimen or potential record fish, or a sustained run of luck. Includes built-in compass, range-finder and pub-detector.

Reinforced anti-missile crown wards off bricks thrown by steamy-jealous members of the opposition team. Easily converted to a carrier bag when the wife asks you to call for 10 lb of spuds on the way home.

Knock, knock.
Who's there?
Hiram.
Hiram who?
They didn't sell rods on the pier, so I had to Hiram.

The Welly Suspender

Keeps your welly socks upright and un-rumpled. No longer will they slip down into the toe of the welly, leaving you at the mercy of the elements and causing you to hobble to the pub. No longer will you have to remove your wellies in front of your mates, giving them the excuse for ribald jokes, rushing out of pong-range, or throwing up.

Easily converted to catapult for long-range groundbaiting operations, dissuading ducks or pinging snotty-nosed urchins who are throwing bricks into your swim.

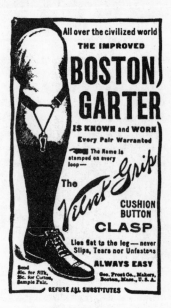

The Snugazabug Winter Outfit

Never again fear winter's chill in the Snugazabug Winter Outfit, consisting of:

Three thermal vests
Two pairs long johns
One pair short johns
Three pairs thermal welly socks
Two pullies

Yak-hide anorak with extra-size inside pockets to take hot water bottles
Bearskin bobbly hat incorporating ear muffs and medicated nose cosy
Pair fleecy-lined sheepskin gloves on string
All-in-one reindeer-hide boots and trousers incorporating duck-down foot muffs and Thermogene willy warmer

WARNING: This is the outfit for the real he-man. Wearing it, anybody under 17 stone and not in regular weight training finds it impossible to stand up. If in doubt, consult your doctor or wear heavy-duty truss.

The Two-In-One Sunshade and Brolly

Come rain, come shine, protects the angler from the elements and low-flying pigeons, while leaving both hands free for baiting up, casting, reeling in, bum-scratching, nose-picking and taking the tops off beer cans.

It's a Fact

Splashing Out

Fishing in the River Tiber in Rome must have improved no end in 69 AD when a sizeable attraction was thrown in in the shape of the Emperor Vitellius. He was a notorious glutton, spending more than £1,200 a day just on food. Apart from the usual larks' tongues in aspic and the odd boar's head, he used to put away a daily snack of 1,000 oysters. After being done to death by the Roman citizens, who were probably peeved about having to pay for it all, he was dumped in the Tiber 'as food for the fishes', so becoming the first recorded and most expensive example of high-protein groundbait.

Great Angling Loonies

Pass the Earwigs . . .

British naturalist Frank Buckland (1826–1880) had a few strange tastes in food, such as elephant's trunk soup, rhinoceros steaks, roast giraffe, Japanese sea slug and mice on buttered toast. One of his failures was broiled porpoise head: he said he could not stop it tasting like an oil lamp wick. He wasn't keen on earwigs, either: reckoned they tasted 'terribly bitter'.

Buckland was a founder member of the Society for the Acclimatisation of Animals in the United Kingdom, an organisation devoted to breeding everything from ostriches to elephants in the UK as additions to the nation's food supplies.

He took the same enthusiasm to his job as Inspector of Salmon Fisheries in 1867. One of his first innovations was the setting up of salmon ladders at weirs to help salmon reach their spawning grounds. At one difficult spot he left a notice telling the salmon: 'Go downstream, take the first turn to the right and you will find good travelling water upstream and no jumping required.' To make sure the salmon didn't think it was a hoax, he initialled the notice.

An indication of how much he threw himself into his work was the fact that his luggage always smelt strongly of fish, so much so that he was usually given a carriage to himself on the train.

His dedication brought him to an untimely end on 19 December 1880. He never recovered from standing for hours up to his chest in icy water in January 1878, trying to get hold of salmon eggs for a special shipment to New Zealand. Fish were on his mind to the end. In his will he wrote: 'God is so good, so very good

Buckland admiring two well-fed little monkeys, who would have been very worried if they'd known his tastes in food.

to little fishes. I do not believe he would let their inspector suffer shipwreck at last. I am going on a long journey where I think I shall see a great many curious animals . . . this journey I must go alone.'

Great Angling Traditions

Barring the Way

Barring the way at weddings is an old Scottish and North Country custom in which the way is barred for bride and groom until the best man has shelled out some cash for drinks. At a ceremony in Eyemouth, Berwickshire, the way was barred by fishing creels until the cash was handed over.

It is unreliably reported that the custom originated as the one sure way of getting a drink out of the groom. Or to remind him that he's booked for a match after the reception.

It's a Fact

A last roundup of fascinating facts you'll wonder how you ever lived without.

No Sex, Please, We're Oysters

Ironic that the oyster, long renowned as an aphrodisiac, should have its own sex life curtailed. During their breeding season, oysters don't taste as good as they might, so genetic scientists have bred a sexless strain that stays fat and tastes nice all the year round.

What a Shocker

The electric eel of South American rivers can discharge shocks of up to 600 volts to kill prey and ward off predators. (The voltage in British homes is a mere 240.) The shock lasts less than a second, and it takes the fish an hour to recharge its batteries, but it gives enough power to light more than a dozen electric light bulbs.

Bigger Than Any of Us

The biggest living thing in the sea is not a fish at all, but a mammal. The blue whale has been known to reach 110 feet in length and weigh almost 200 tons. Even a baby blue is massive. At birth, the calf weighs 10 tons – twice as much as a full-grown African elephant.

Winter Warmers

Eskimos use fridges to keep their fish in – not to keep it frozen, but to stop it from freezing rock-solid as it would do if it were left outside.

Out of This World

A company in New York is doing a roaring trade in the sale of fishing rights – on Venus and Mars. Anglers are paying 10 dollars for each 50-yard fishing stretch. 'Business is booming,' said a spokesman. 'We're selling 70 a day.'

What's Cooking?

Most people are familiar with cooking methods for salmon and trout. But what about coarse fish? Coarse fish were eaten a lot in Britain before the railways provided cheap sea fish, and are still eaten a lot on the continent today.

You may have been lucky enough to get a fish cookery book among your Christmas presents. If not, you could try one of these recipes next time you land a decent-sized fish.

Carp

Take out the guts with the gills and the head. Wash the carp clean in salt and water, then soak the fish for an hour in a fresh brine solution.

FRIED CARP

Open out the fish and pat it well dry. Cover in seasoned flour, fry each side in butter until browned. Serve with melted butter or anchovy sauce.

Or:

Open out the fish, cover it with egg and bread-crumbs and fry each side in butter until browned. Pour a cup of sour cream over the fish and simmer gently. Serve with boiled potatoes and sprinkle with chopped fennel and parsley.

BAKED CARP

Clean as above. Place the fish in ovenproof dish with butter. Bake in moderate oven (355°F, Regulo 4) until flesh leaves the bone easily. Or allow 10 minutes to the pound up to 4 lb, and 5 minutes thereafter. Cover with greased paper for the first three quarters of cooking time, then remove to allow top to brown.

Gudgeon

Wash in salted water. Leave the scales and heads on, but remove the fins and gills. Clean out the intestines through the gill apertures. Because of their small size, you need several gudgeon for a decent meal.

FRIED GUDGEON

Gudgeon are delicious fried. Roll in seasoned flour and fry in oil with minced shallot, parsley, thyme, bay leaf and clove of garlic. Serve hot, with oil and herbs as sauce, or cold.

Or:

Fry in shallow fat or butter with sprinkling of *fines herbes* (chives, parsley, tarragon, chervil).

Or:

Coat in seasoned egg and breadcrumbs and fry in deep fat or oil. In France, the head and tail are left uncoated, so that the cooked fish appear to be wearing a breadcrumb overcoat. Known as *en manchon* (in a muff), this is very *cordon bleu* and very off-putting. Worse than whitebait, the way they look at you.

Perch

Perch scales are tough. Plunging the fish into boiling water for two or three minutes makes de-scaling easier.

FRIED PERCH

Score each side several times and season with salt and pepper. Fry gently in butter on both sides. That's all you need. Delicious.

PERCH IN BUTTER

Put 3 oz butter in a saucepan. Add some skinned, sliced tomatoes and minced shallot. Season cleaned perch with lemon juice, salt and garlic. Place in saucepan and add chopped parsley and basil. Simmer slowly on low heat until ready. Serve with the liquid as a sauce.

BOILED PERCH

To 1¾ pints of water, add 2 tablespoons salt, 1 dessertspoonful vinegar. Add also parsley, thyme and bay leaf. Boil for 10 to 15 minutes. Serve with boiled potatoes and melted butter sauce, flavoured with chopped parsley and lemon juice.

Pike

'Your pike must not be a small one,' wrote Izaak Walton. 'That is, it must be more than half a yard, and should be bigger.'

Half a yard (18 in) is probably under the takeaway weight for the water these days, weighing just over 2 lb, so think quite a bit bigger. A seven-pounder is not an impossible size for cooking (on Mona's Scale it brings you to about 28½ in). Lots of head on pike, anyway . . .

After the pike is gutted, it should be soaked in salt water for 12 hours; otherwise it will taste muddy.

Try pike steamed, with parsley sauce. Or:

PIKE STEAKS

Cut the cleaned fish into steaks. Sprinkle the steaks with lemon juice to keep them white. For every 2 lb of fish, melt 4 oz butter in a shallow, ovenproof dish and lay the steaks on it. Arrange anchovy fillets on each steak. Pour about half a teacupful of sour cream over the steaks, and sprinkle with 2 oz fine white breadcrumbs. Bake in a moderate oven (355°F, Regulo 4) for about 25 minutes.

POACHED PIKE WITH WINE

Place fillets of pike in a lightly-buttered ovenproof dish, with a little chopped onion, salt, pepper and lemon juice. Cover the steaks with dry white wine. Put a lid on the dish and place in a very moderate oven (335°F, Regulo 3). Poach gently for 15-20 minutes or until finished. To serve, reduce the strained cooking liquor, thicken with egg yolk, butter and cream, and pour over the fish.

Roach

Not the gastronomic thrill of a lifetime, and too many bones for comfort. But you can try seasoning it and grilling it with butter, or frying it with bacon.

Tench

Scald in boiling water to help de-scaling.

BAKED TENCH

Clean and scale the fish, sprinkle it with lemon juice, and leave for an hour before cooking. Put in shallow, ovenproof dish with 3 oz melted butter. Season with salt, pepper and small minced onion. Cover with buttered paper. Bake gently for about 30 minutes at 335°F, Regulo 3. Make a white sauce. When fish is cooked, add cooking liquid to sauce. To every half-pint of sauce, add tablespoonful of lemon juice and tablespoonful of chopped pickled gherkins.

FRIED TENCH, FRENCH STYLE

Clean tench and dust with seasoned flour. Fry in olive oil and butter, adding small quantities of minced leek, shallot or garlic, chopped parsley and breadcrumbs.

Barbel, Bream, Chub and Rudd

Don't bother.